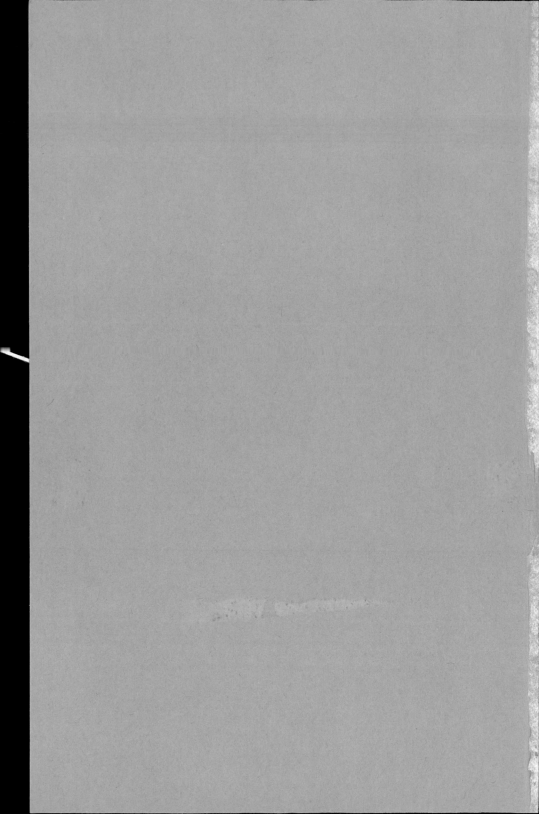

A
KNIGHT
AT THE
OPERA

A KNIGHT AT THE OPERA

Sir Rudolf Bing

G. P. PUTNAM'S SONS
NEW YORK

Library of Congress Cataloging in Publication Data

Bing, Rudolf, Sir, date.
A knight at the opera.

Includes index.
1. Bing, Rudolf, Sir, 1902-   . 2. Impresarios
—Biography. I. Title.
ML429.B52A33   782.1′092′4 [B]   81-10534
ISBN 0-399-12653-8   AACR2

Designed by Bernard Schleifer

Printed in the United States of America

To *my beloved wife, Nina*

ACKNOWLEDGMENTS

I WOULD LIKE TO express deep appreciation for all the help friends and foes have given me in writing this book. And, in particular, to the public who, during twenty-two years, even though many may have disapproved, on the whole have supported my efforts.

I don't know how to thank Garson Kanin, an old friend and outstanding writer who gave his valuable time and his sparkling wit to introduce this book. Also, warm thanks to John Gutman for his loyalty through a long life of friendship.

I would also like to thank Dr. Howard B. Gottlieb, archivist of Mugar Memorial Library at Boston University, who kindly agreed to store my papers; Mrs. John DeWitt Peltz and her staff in the archives of the Metropolitan Opera for the untiring efforts to be helpful; Diane Reverand, my editor, for her understanding and welcome advice; Dick Boehm, agent and friend who encouraged and helped me in every step of the way.

INTRODUCTION

IN HIS REMARKABLY candid, fascinating, and revealing memoir, *5,000 Nights at the Opera*, Sir Rudolf Bing took us inside the wonderland of the world of opera. We were, in turn, amused, entertained, shocked, thrilled, surprised, and inspired.

Now he has gracefully agreed to continue the saga. No one living is more qualified to do so. For surely, Rudolf Bing was the outstanding figure of opera in America for almost twenty-five years. He came to the Metropolitan Opera Company in 1950 and, in an astonishingly short time, transformed a moribund, mediocre institution into a vital, exciting, invaluable part of our cultural life.

My personal involvement with this unique and impressive impresario began in a small, dingy, dusty room hidden away in the labyrinth of the old Metropolitan Opera House.

Mr. Rudolf Bing, the newly appointed General Manager, had sent for me. I could not imagine why. I had heard of him, of course, during a residency in London. I had been told that during World War II he had worked as a floorwalker at Peter Jones's department store. I had been enchanted by the Glyndebourne Festival which he had managed, to say nothing of the great Edinburgh Festival. But what could he possibly want with me? I soon found out.

Seated behind an ancient, rickety table—the handsome, elegant, humorous, urbane gentleman began to speak.

He explained that he hoped to bring new life to his planned productions by engaging experienced stage directors to put them on, thus freeing the company from the domination of conductors, who, in his opinion, often neglected stagecraft in their zeal to protect every grace note of the score.

I was but one of several directors who had been suggested. Among the others were Margaret Webster, Alfred Lunt, Joseph L. Mankiewicz, Elia Kazan, Joshua Logan, and Tyrone Guthrie.

I told Mr. Bing at once that I was honored and flattered to be invited, but that I did not consider myself qualified, and that, in any case, I was not available, having entered into negotiations for the assignment of directing the original Broadway production of Frank Loesser's *Guys and Dolls*.

"I don't know the work," said Mr. Bing. "But surely it cannot compare with Strauss's *Fledermaus*, which I would like you to do here."

"I can't," I said.

"Think on it," said Mr. Bing. "I would like to do it in English. Who would be a good lyricist? Would you consider writing a new libretto?"

I was bemused. Could it be that this man, who spoke English so beautifully, understood it so indifferently? We parted, politely, each making vague remarks.

"I need a new suit of clothes," he said, suddenly. "Where should I go?"

"Brooks Brothers," I said, aimlessly.

The next day he phoned.

"For the third act part of Frosch," he said, "we should have a great comedian. Danny Kaye? Milton Berle? Ed Wynn? Someone said Bert Lahr."

"Any one of those," I said. "And to direct, may I suggest George S. Kaufman or George Abbott?"

"Thank you," said Mr. Bing.

A long letter arrived from him a few days later, importuning.

I replied with an even longer one declining the offer firmly and finally.

He invited me to lunch the following week. "Just to talk," he said.

We lunched and talked. He never left the subject of *Fledermaus*.

"For me," he said, "it is one of the most important and rare works in the entire operatic repertoire."

"Why is that?" I asked, amazed.

"Because," he replied, "it is great *and* light. That puts it in a category almost by itself. Great *and* light. Richard

Tucker will sing Alfred divinely. And I have Patrice Munsel for Adele. And we have Ljuba Welitsch for Rosalinda. And you have your choice of any members of the company for the remaining parts. It will be the glory of the season."

I noted the subtle shift from the "I" to "we" to "you." I was being hypnotized.

"Mr. Bing," I said, "you're most persuasive and you make it extremely tempting, but I'm not going to do it because I don't think I'm capable. So thank you, but no."

Two days later he phoned. "Will you reconsider?" he asked.

"I have," I replied, "and the answer is still no. The job scares me."

"I see," said Mr. Bing. "Very well."

Some months later, I found myself in one of the large rehearsal studios on the mezzanine floor of the old Met, surrounded by a glorious cast singing through the first rehearsal of *Fledermaus*, which I was directing with the redoubtable Dr. Fritz Reiner conducting. I had also written a new libretto and Mr. Bing had convinced Howard Dietz to write the lyrics. Howard, too, had begun with a firm refusal.

I was somewhat discomfited to note that Mr. Bing was not present. It took some time before I realized that Mr. Bing was *never* around—until he was needed. Then, he always appeared, as if summoned by unseen, unknown forces, to deal with the crisis at hand. To this day, I have not discovered the solution to this mystery. I am not the only one who has observed the phenomenon. Many members of the casts and crews were equally aware of this genie-like magic.

During the second week of rehearsals, I was working alone with the principals and explained that in the second act "orgy" scene, they would all be lying about on enormous pillows in the ballroom set.

"No, no!" said a voice behind me. I turned and saw Fritz Reiner. He continued, speaking to the company. "You will be *standing* and facing the audience and keeping your eyes on *me*. Very hard, this ensemble, to keep together."

"Just a minute, Maestro—" I began.

"Singers cannot sing lying down," he said. "Sometimes not even standing up. Listen to Papa."

"Would you be willing to try it, Maestro, because otherwise—"

"No," Reiner said.

"Take a break, ladies and gentlemen," said Rudolf Bing, who had suddenly materialized, seemingly out of thin air.

The company left.

"Please sit down, gentlemen," said Bing.

We sat, too close to one another, I thought.

Reiner attacked at once. "I have conducted many operas," he said, "hundreds. This boy has done none. Why should I argue and discuss? They will stand, not lie down."

Mr. Bing turned to me and raised his eyebrows quizzically.

I said, "It's not a matter of them standing or lying down at this point. What matters to me is an understanding of exactly what my position is to be. I'm afraid that as we go on, if the Maestro has the power to veto any ideas I may have, my usefulness to this project will be nil."

Mr. Bing turned to Reiner, wordlessly, and waited.

"It has always been so," said Reiner. "I am responsible. I am the conductor." He looked at me. "You don't tell me how to conduct and I don't tell you how to direct."

"But that's exactly what you *are* doing, Maestro."

"Singers cannot sing lying down. I will not have it."

Mr. Bing rose, bowed slightly, and said, "Thank you, gentlemen."

The company returned and the rehearsal proceeded automatically. Neither Reiner nor I said a word to anyone.

Presently, John Gutman, Mr. Bing's Assistant General Manager appeared and in a few minutes left with Dr. Reiner.

A week later Reiner had been replaced by Eugene Ormandy, who, at his first rehearsal, said to the company, "And for heaven's sake, don't look at *me* all the time. Let me and my orchestra be your accompanist. And as to the staging, let us all try to carry out the director's conception. If he wants you to sing standing on your heads, let us try it. If it doesn't work, we will reverse you."

For the drunken jailer, Frosch, in act three, I devised stage business which had to do with his finding bottles of whiskey hidden away in every part of the set. Desk drawers, wastebaskets, behind pictures, in the prompter's box, vases, and so on. At one point, I suggested to

Jack Gilford, who was playing Frosch, to come down to the footlights, beckon to the tuba player to stand, take a bottle out of the horn, swig it, and drop it back into the horn. It seemed to play well, but at the first rehearsal with the orchestra, we discovered, to our dismay, that there was no tuba in the *Fledermaus* orchestration.

"Too bad, Jack," I said. "Cut the bit."

"Not at all," said Mr. Bing, suddenly at my side. "We shall put the tuba in."

"But he has no part," said Ormandy.

"Let him sit, then," said Mr. Bing, "until the joke."

Thus it was that for the more than fifteen years that *Fledermaus* remained in the Met repertoire, a tuba player was engaged for every performance—simply to sit until the joke in act three.

I relate these incidents only as examples of Rudolf Bing's method of administration.

Think of the number of crises and difficult situations he must have faced in his twenty-two years' tenure as General Manager of the Metropolitan Opera Company. He was not always popular with some members of the company, but what General Manager ever has been? He often irritated the press. This, too, is traditional.

What he set out to do was to develop the finest opera company in the world and in this, in time, he succeeded.

Rudolf Bing was deeply involved in the planning and construction of the new Metropolitan Opera House at Lincoln Center. During one of the meetings of the Lincoln Center Board, it was announced that a Mrs. Vivian Beaumont would underwrite the construction of the legitimate theater with the proviso that it be called "The Vivian Beaumont Theater." It was generally thought that this was an awkward name for the theater, but the Board was told that this condition was absolute. While everyone was thinking it over, Mr. Bing looked up and said, "Would she settle for calling it 'The Old Viv'?"

His feud with the great Maria Callas and her manager-husband was highly publicized. But in the end, Maria Callas said, "Despite our differences, he was a great manager."

He once invited her to sing the role of the Queen of the Night in *The Magic Flute*.

"It doesn't make sense," she said, "for you to pay such a large fee for such a small part."

"I have the solution!" said Bing. "Reduce your fee."

I was once a guest in his box at the new Met and saw a revival of one of the productions that had been done six or seven years earlier. At the end, I said to him, "Well, it's not what it used to be." To which he replied, "It never was."

Martin Bernheimer, music critic of *The Los Angeles Times*, called him "the most powerful autocrat of our generation."

The superlative impresario was ever loyal to his company. When, in Chicago, the formidable Claudia Cassidy, objecting to the absence of a few of the principal singers, referred to the company as "a bunch of stumblebums," Bing canceled all subsequent Chicago bookings.

When the company played at the Paris Opera and some members of the French press criticized Roberta Peters, Bing responded, "Miss Peters may have had a bad night, but the Paris Opera has had a bad century."

One of his stars with a bad throat tried for a high C, which cracked. Bing commented, "It's like a woman wearing a very low-cut dress. You're not sure if it's more rude to look or not to look." The cracked note was never mentioned.

Although he spent the most important part of his working life in the United States, he was knighted by Queen Elizabeth in 1971. In addition to this, he was awarded the highest honor that the Austrian government has to offer civilians. He was also given the Cross of Chevalier de la Légion d'Honneur; the Commander's Cross of the Order of Merit of the Federal Republic of Germany; and the rank of Commander in the Order of Merit of the Republic of Italy. But I, for one, am certain that he would gladly trade any one of these honors for a splendid production of an opera at the Metropolitan.

The present work is a souvenir, a gift to us, on his eightieth birthday. The number has no significance. Mr. Bing, Rudolf Bing, Sir Rudolf, Rudi, is—like his vision, his aspiration, and his achievements—ageless.

GARSON KANIN

A
KNIGHT
AT THE
OPERA

PROLOGUE

IN MY LAST YEARS at the
Met, I could hardly wait to get out. Now that I am out, I
miss it every day.

I could hardly wait to get to my office and find my
desk loaded with problems of every kind. The tenor of
tonight's performance was sick and canceled. The
soprano of this morning's dress rehearsal would not go
on unless she was permitted to wear her own costume
which in no way matched the others. Another prominent singer asked for a release to do a concert in
Cleveland on the day before an important premiere
here. I could not possibly allow him to fly about in
winter, catch cold or have a five-hour delay on arrival at
the airport.

These were the immediate or "first hour" crises as we called them. The tenor had to be persuaded to stay or a replacement had to be found, which might involve overseas calls if no suitable replacement could be found at home. The soprano had to be coaxed to do the rehearsal with the promise that the tailor would do the best he could to meet her wishes. At this point I would be asked to come to the stage where the director and the designer were having a fight as to where a particular staircase should lead. Needless to say, the early crises produced later ones and there was always the performance, which produced many a crisis on many a night.

I no longer face these crises though I face a different sort. The Met has changed. So have I.

My first book, *5000 Nights at the Opera,* was more or less about my professional career: the early days, Glyndebourne, Edinburgh and, for twenty-two years, the Met. As I reread my book after many years, it is obvious that I had left out incidents I had wished to put in—not to mention the passages I put in but wish I had left out.

I made statements I don't really believe today. But in some cases, I made statements that, if anything, I believe more today. I cannot and will not write a nasty or gossipy book, easy as it might be. While there will be few repeats in themes, these themes will have variations.

It was clear in my first book that I was never close to artists in general. But I still occasionally meet singers from the Met, usually while they are on the way to the bank. They look around carefully to see if anyone can see them. If they don't catch sight of a familiar face, they embrace me.

The days of excitement are gone. And I miss them. But at least I am spared Franco Corelli's dog. He was so well trained that he would sit in his master's dressing room waiting for anybody who might reach for the paycheck. Then he would bite.

ONE

After the 1961 STRIKE, which, of course, caused damage to the Met—and even though it certainly was not my fault—I offered my resignation. The Board, if they so desired, could have installed a new manager. I just felt I couldn't go on. I wrote to Tony Bliss, then the President of the Board, as follows:

Dear Tony:

Events have moved a little faster than I have anticipated. As they also helped me to clear my own mind, I feel it is only right that I should immediately give you some basic information which will enable you and your col-

27

leagues on the Board to consider next steps necessary.

It is not just a form, but completely sincere, if I say that, even after all these years I feel deeply honored and flattered that you have suggested extending my contract. I am desperately sorry, but I feel quite certain now that this would be a mistake: consequently, please do not count on my services as General Manager beyond the expiration date of my present contract.

As I said, this information will now make it possible for you to get to grips with the problem of succession at the Metropolitan. Needless to say that if it is felt that my advice or consultations with me can be of any help, you know that you can completely and unreservedly count on my availability.

This is not the letter or the time to get into any emotional explanations, but you know, of course, that the Metropolitan Opera has for all these years been virtually my life, and you also know how happily and gratefully I enjoy the most pleasant collaboration with you and the Board. It is, therefore, only natural that the future well-being and success of the organization is extremely close to my heart, and I will do everything I can to be helpful.

If, indeed, you and the Board should come up with a solution somewhat approaching what we discussed the other day where I might continue in some sort of consultative activity, I would be very glad to explore such a possibility further if you should so desire.

With kind regards,

As it happened, they declined.

And I again wrote to my Board of Directors in October 1968 with thoughts of who should succeed me as General Manager.

That I was able to arrive in New York, November of 1949, and plan the next season at the Met is quite different from the present time when one has to plan years ahead hoping to be not too late in booking the artists of your choice.

In any event, I recently found this memo to the Board, of which the following are excerpts:

Anybody appointed to succeed me in June 1972 would have to be available at the Metropolitan in New York at the latest during the 1971–1972 season, that is from approximately August or September 1971. Even then, operatic matters being what they are, the season 1972–1973 would have to be to all intents and purposes preplanned by me. If a new General Manager would be expected to be really responsible for planning his first season entirely on his own, he would have to be available for at least two years ahead of time, that is, during the two seasons 1970–1971 and 1971–1972, which seems not desirable in the interests of both the outgoing and the incoming Manager and consequently not really in the interest of the House, which would have for two years both a "lame-duck" manager and a "not-yet-responsible" manager. It seems to me, therefore, desirable to accept the fact that a new Manager would have more or less to take over his first season as preplanned by me and start being really responsible with his second season. This situation would naturally change entirely if the new Manager were to come from the existing team, which would make for an easy transition and would make it possible for the new man to begin planning his first season.

Now allow me to deal briefly with the type of management the Board might consider. I am aware that various forms of a "Troika" or a "paid president," etc., are being discussed. Permit me to say that I urgently warn against any of these variations. One of the fascinations of the theatrical profession is the inextricable relationship between artistic, financial and human elements. There is no artistic decision that is without human and financial consequences. There is no financial decision that does not reflect itself in artistic and human terms. It is impossible to departmentalize and it is imperative that final decisions on all matters rest in one hand.

Naturally one would expect a man of the quality to hold the job of General Manager of the world's most important lyric theater to be able not only to delegate but also to listen to advice and, in nine out of ten cases, to reach agreement with his collaborators. But in the one case where opinions differ, it must be the General Manager who decides. Naturally, it doesn't matter what you call the man. If you want to call him a paid president, that is fine. But then the paid president had better be a professional in a position to form his own opinions and decisions on the thousand and one problems that every day will come to his desk: from casting to deciding on priority of stage time between competing and conflicting directors, from budget allocations to whether and how to discipline irresponsible stars. . . .

As it happens the Metropolitan never had a music director—and apparently did not do too badly. There is at present no music director in Vienna, in Milan or in Munich. There is one in London (George Solti), who is about to leave. I am unaware whether and how he might be replaced. But the Manager of Covent Garden (Sir David Webster) when he took over just after the war, came from a department store in Liverpool. His theatrical and artistic experience was nil and he was then totally dependent on the advice of a music director. The first one, a little more than twenty years ago, was Karl Rankl. Then, for a while, Rafael Kubelik and for the past two years, Solti. Sir David is a smooth and skilled negotiator and perhaps has been lucky never to allow a real difference of opinion to develop. Had it developed, I guess his would have been the right to decide and had his decision been against Solti's I suspect there might have been trouble.

At the Metropolitan—at least during the nearly nineteen years of my term, such trouble has never arisen. I have always listened carefully to my collaborators. We have not always agreed, but in most cases, I have either accepted their view or they agreed to mine. But in the rare cases when we could not agree, everyone in the House has without question and with complete loyalty accepted my decision. The General Manager is and must be totally responsible, and that alone gives the house his stamp for better or for worse. With a "Troika" or any other form of coequal management, you have nobody responsible and, as a result, a faceless house.

I am not saying that the possibility of a music director with certain prerogatives could not be considered. But I am saying that if that was difficult thirty and twenty years ago, it is more difficult now, when conductors of distinction are few and far between and less and less inclined to devote sufficient time to one organization.

Also, suppose you do get a man of Karajan's standing to become your music director. You will find it more difficult to get any other conductor of distinction to the House because they will suspect—rightly or wrongly—that the music director will arrange for himself the most interesting works, the best casts and the most rehearsals . . . such was the case in Vienna under Karajan as general manager. While under the present arrangement—look at this season—the Met will enjoy the services of Karajan, Boehm, Krips, Abbado, Mehta, Colin Davis, Molinari-Pradelli, etc. Virtually all operatic conductors of distinction who are available.

My conclusion: there must be *one* head with ultimate power in all spheres, responsible to the Board—as is the case with me. And now allow me to speak a little about *some* of the names that have come up or should come up for consideration.

Kurt Herbert Adler:

For the past ten or more years, General Manager of the San Francisco Opera. In all he has been twenty-five years—formerly as chorus master, then as assistant to the General Manager—with that Company. Of course Adler is a man of great operatic knowledge and experience, used to dealing with artists of international caliber.

However, I don't think that he is more than five years younger than I am which means to say that by 1972 he will be around sixty-five years of age, which I suspect may eliminate him from the list of possibles.

Julius Rudel:

May be at least ten or twelve years younger. Also a man of great experience though on a totally different level. Rudel is a fine musician and a good conductor. He is too well known in New York to require me to give a more detailed description of his qualifications. Whether after nearly twenty-five years with the City Center operation, he could adjust himself to the different world of the Metropolitan Opera is hard to judge.

As I said, he is of course an extremely well known New York musical figure and, in line with the general attitude of praising the underdog, very much the blue-eyed boy of the New York music critics. How long the honeymoon would last I cannot foresee. But, of course, he is a man who should be considered.

Carol Fox:

Miss Fox, in my view, has considerable qualifications as an Opera Manager. She has for many years, first jointly with Larry Kelly and after a break with him, alone, been responsible for the Lyric Opera in Chicago, which has developed into a respectable Company, working at least vocally on an international level. We share many international artists with her. She seems able to plan well in advance, has as far as I know confidence from her Board, and has, in serious situations, shown leadership and courage. Whether at this stage she would consider leaving Chicago and moving to New York, I do not know. She is a woman of considerable ability.

Rolf Liebermann:

Manager of the Hamburg State Opera. I think his name came up on the occasion of Hamburg's visit to Lincoln Center in the summer of 1967. He also was under consideration for the Vienna post, but eventually according to my information, signed for Hamburg for five years, which might make him available around 1972. I would think Liebermann nine or ten years younger than I. That means he would be approaching sixty in 1972 if my guess is correct.

He is a man of considerable ability. In my view his musical taste and production tendencies are totally wrong for the New York public. He goes all out for contemporary opera and for ultra-modern productions which, no doubt, would create a love affair with the press and at the same time disaster with the subscribers and the box office.

I think we have to face the taste and desires of the overwhelming majority of Metropolitan Opera subscribers and patrons. It would take a decade or more and immense amounts of money to change these tastes.

Lord Harewood:
I know that he was seen by a number of directors two or three years ago so he is known to some of you and also his background is known. He is very much on the same line as Liebermann except that he has no experience as manager in charge of an opera house. He has experience as a member of the Covent Garden Management and he is, no doubt, a

man of high intelligence and ability. He is one of my successors as Artistic Director of the Edinburgh Festival. I personally have known George Harewood since before the war and rather like him.

Erich Leinsdorf:

Needless to say Erich Leinsdorf is a distinguished conductor who would give the House certainly a degree of musical leadership which may be desirable.

I think Leinsdorf might be seriously considered as a music director if the new General Manager and the Board desire such a position. But from my long and close experience with Leinsdorf I cannot recommend him as General Manager.

I have left to the last two names which perhaps should have been at the head of my list: Herman Krawitz and Robert Herman. I don't think that in all my more than forty years of professional activities I have ever had more able collaborators. They are both men of superior intelligence, unflagging devotion to their work and to this organization—phenomenal workers and of outstanding ability in their respective spheres.

Robert Herman, I think, would make an outstanding General Manager. He is just young enough to be available for a long tenure. He has now for twelve or fourteen years stood at the absolute center of the Met's Management. He could take over without a moment's hesitation. He has qualities of leadership. You may find that not everybody in the House likes him. I am quite sure not everybody in the House likes me.

Bob Herman is the man who nine times out of ten has to say "no" and in that position, you don't easily win popularity contests.

There is no question that Bob Herman has some drawbacks—who hasn't?—but men rise to their higher goals and grow with their responsibilities and he has the intelligence to learn, the intelligence to listen and the intelligence to take advice. I think he is a first-rate man.

I think he is probably the only one who might succeed in getting Herman Krawitz to remain with him. I frankly think the organization could not hope for a better team than Bob Herman as General Manager with Herman Krawitz as Business Manager or General Administrator or some position of that sort.

One thing seems to me to be of paramount importance. That is, that no kind of publicly known action should be taken for my replacement before the union negotiations due to start this spring are completed. I hope the Board will not wish to repeat the mistake of last time when Management was largely sidestepped and an important part of the negotiations were conducted by the then-president of the Board.

If Management, and this means in particular the General Manager, is supposed to take charge of the next round of negotiations, naturally under the guidance and under instructions from the Board, it would be disastrous if the unions would feel that they are already dealing with a "lame duck."

But I stayed. And there was a strike that postponed the 1969–1970 season until December 29.

I am happy to say Bob Herman made a fantastic career as General Manager of the Miami Opera Company. He, as far as I know, turned his company into the one and only one in the black.

When I think of the enormous success that Herman Krawitz makes with his various enterprises, including the executive directorship of the

American Ballet Theater, I feel a certain pride that these two men, whom I picked as principal assistants and who worked for me nineteen years, both made personal successes after they left the Met with me.

The third of my closest collaborators was John Gutman. In fact I had known John long before I came to the United States. He was a music critic in Berlin and came to Darmstadt while I was there. When I joined the Met, I felt I needed one friend from the past whom I could trust completely. John, of course, has a strong musical background. I invited him to join my management, and twenty-two years of happy collaboration followed.

In regard to my closest collaborators, in twenty-two years, not a single one was ever fired by me. Charles Riecker and Paul Jaretzski, surely two of the most valuable collaborators for all of us in Management stayed on with the Met after I left.

Also, for all my twenty-two years, there was Francis Robinson. He was at the Met when I came and stayed until his untimely death in 1980.

As it happened only a very few weeks before, I met Francis on the street and hardly recognized him. He looked frighteningly sick. We spoke a few words. This turned out to be our last meeting.

Francis's overriding quality was his ability to make friends with people, to tell always the right story at the right moment, and so he was the ideal person for handling public relations.

He loved the Met. In fact, it was his life. I can hardly imagine anyone passing Francis's office knowing he is no longer there. All of us will miss him and keep him warmly in our memory.

TWO

A

S MY DAYS OF twenty-two years as General Manager of the Metropolitan Opera were finally drawing to a close in 1972, Goeran Gentele, my appointed successor, was observing the activities of the Opera House as I had observed Edward Johnson twenty-three years before.

I appreciated his warm and cordial letter when he returned to Stockholm during his observation year, thanking me for "very fine cooperation."

I remarked to someone, "I wish him well, poor dear. He doesn't know what he's in for." Indeed he did not. A few weeks later he died in a dreadful car accident.

Gentele was, of course, planning his first seasons as I was wrapping up my last with the usual problems. I had planned five new productions for this last season. One of them, *The Daughter of the Regiment,* was borrowed from the Royal Opera House in London. With Joan Sutherland, Luciano Pavarotti and Ljuba Welitsch in a small character part, conducted by Richard Bonynge, it was good fun. *Der Freischütz* was one of the less remarkable productions. *Pelléas et Mélisande* enjoyed poetic sets by Desmond Heeley. Paul-Emile Deiber directed and the cast included Judith Blegen, Barry McDaniel, Thomas Stewart, Giorgio Tozzi and Lili Chookasian, conducted by Colin Davis.

The high points of the season were the two new productions of *Tristan und Isolde* and *Otello,* my last production. *Tristan* with Birgit Nilsson and Jess Thomas was no doubt one of the most beautiful productions of this masterpiece at the Metropolitan. Schneider-Siemssen's designs and August Everding's direction lifted the performance to a rare level of beauty.

I was equally proud of *Otello.* With Karl Boehm conducting, Franco Zeffirelli as designer and director, and James McCracken, Teresa Zylis-Gara and Sherrill Milnes heading the cast, I felt I left the Met a production it could long remember and use.

For my farewell evening, I planned to produce the second act of *Fledermaus* with the traditional "party" to introduce the guest artists. Indeed,

Beverly Sills used this idea in her farewell as a singer. My problem was that Birgit Nilsson was scheduled to end the program and she wanted to sing either the Immolation Scene or the final scene of *Salome*. I really didn't think that either was too cheerful in the *Fledermaus* setting. Nor did I wish to lose Nilsson. We finally discarded *Fledermaus* and produced a Gala Concert. It was sold out for months.

That April 22 began like any other day. I walked Pip, my beloved little dachshund, in the park. I had my usual breakfast and proceeded to the Met. My desk was filled with letters and telegrams. One message was from a former usher and another from Herbert von Karajan which read:

On this day I feel particularly close to you as man, as artist and as initiator of a great time at the Metropolitan Opera. Your life's work will not be forgotten and I look forward, hopefully, to seeing you soon. All the best also from my wife. Yours, Herbert von Karajan.

I commented: "My God. I have arrived." But I was touched that this was not merely a formal wire but a warm, personal message.

I also received a letter from then President Nixon which read:

Dear Sir Rudolf:

This evening is a special and nostalgic occasion for every opera lover, as it marks the last time a performance at the Metropolitan is being given under your inspired leadership.

For all of us, your twenty-two years at the helm of the world's greatest opera house have been a brilliant chapter in our cultural history. The list of your achievements during these two decades is seemingly endless, but among the most significant have been your successful efforts in bringing an ever-increasing number of American and Canadian singers to the stage, enlisting the talents of many distinguished black artists, and guiding the relocation of the Met to its magnificent home at the Lincoln Center.

Through all these splendid accomplishments, you have never lost sight of the Met's principal goal—to present the finest in opera with the highest standards of perfection. Your stewardship of this national and, indeed, international cultural institution has been superb, and I am delighted to extend my warmest congratulations and appreciation for all you have done to enrich and expand our operatic heritage.

With my best wishes,

Sincerely,
RICHARD NIXON

Standees assembled during the preceding night. As it became quite clear there would be many more than the standing room would hold, they drew a lottery system. I got there early in the morning and offered to do the lottery myself. We put all their numbers in a large bowl and I drew the numbers. Everyone whose number was drawn presented it to the box office where they got the tickets—as my guests. I paid for them all.

The afternoon broadcast of April 22 was *Don Carlo,* the opera that had opened my regime. When asked why I chose this opera, I remarked that it was perhaps for sentimental reasons to close the circle. It was close to my heart. I even had two singers from that first performance in the cast. Cesare Siepi, who made his Metropolitan debut on my first opening night, once again sang his distinguished portrayal of King Philip. Lucine Amara, who long since had become one of our leading sopranos, graciously consented to recreate her debut role—the brief offstage role of the celestial voice. The production was the same, designed by Rolf Gérard and directed by Margaret Webster. Among the other singers of this broadcast were Montserrat Caballé, Grace Bumbry, Frederica von Stade, Franco Corelli, Sherrill Milnes and John Macurdy. Not too bad a cast. They were all in excellent voice.

I was on the air during the two intermissions and the host was Cyril Ritchard. Cyril had become a friend over the years, having directed *The Barber of Seville, The Tales of Hoffmann* and *The Marriage of Figaro* for me. He also directed a charming Offenbach operetta, *La Périchole,* in which he played and sang a leading part.

We always said he was the only artist engaged at the Met in spite of his voice.

Cyril was always witty and amusing. He helped me get over the sentiment on this occasion.

The evening Gala began at 8:00 P.M. and ended well after 1:00 A.M. Let me just list the artists in the order they participated:

Roberta Peters, Sherrill Milnes, Teresa Stratas, Thomas Stewart, Paul Plishka, Ruggero Raimondi, Anna Moffo, Martina Arroyo, Joan Sutherland, Luciano Pavarotti, Gail Robinson, Cornell MacNeil, Dorothy Kirsten, Fernando Corena, Ezio Flagello, Montserrat Caballé, Placido Domingo, Grace Bumbry, Régine Crespin, Mario Sereni, Lucine Amara, Enrico Di Giuseppe, Cesare Siepi, Raymond Gniewek (concertmaster), Richard Tucker, Robert Merrill, Leontyne Price, Regina Resnik, Gabriella Tucci, Irene Dalis, John Macurdy, James McCracken, Sándor Kónya, Rosalind Elias, Jerome Hines, Pilar Lorengar, Leonie Rysanek, Jon Vickers, Teresa Zylis-Gara, Franco Corelli and Birgit Nilsson.

The chorus and ballet also performed. The conductors were James Levine, Richard Bonynge, Francesco Molinari-Pradelli, Kurt Adler, Max Rudolf and Karl Boehm. The Met realized an enormous income. It was really a fantastic occasion.

As for that roster, no international opera house could compete, then or now. An hour version of that performance was seen the following week on CBS with Risë Stevens as hostess and the following year in Europe with Lilli Palmer as the hostess.

The next morning, my wife and I left for the Dolomites in the quiet mountain village of Siusi, where we had spent the last twenty-one summers. Pensione Mirabella was a simple but most pleasant place. It became our second home. We had the same apartment every summer with a lovely, closed-in balcony and a little private garden. The

garden was small but big enough for a few armchairs. We could lie in the sun. There was a picture
window looking out on the Schlern, one of the
most beautiful mountains of the Dolomites, which
was almost always snow-covered.

The beautiful air from the mountains was all
around us. It was Hilde Gueden who introduced us
to Siusi, and I am grateful to her. Mr. Egger, the
owner of our pensione, became a friend as the
years went by. When we returned to New York in
September, we could hardly wait for next June. We
loved it. For Nina, who is even more a country
lover than I, these months were perhaps her
happiest.

While Nina and I liked to walk, we didn't like
walking uphill. So Mr. Egger drove us up each
morning. Then we had a perfectly even walk
through the wood, which after an hour and a half
brought us home again. I don't remember that in
all the years we ever changed our walk. It was so
beautiful we didn't need change. Gradually we got
to know all the trees. The squirrels became friends.

Our peace was shattered that summer of 1972
when on July 18 we learned about the tragic and
senseless death of Mr. Gentele. Like the entire
opera world, I was shocked. The normally and
naturally planned succession was immediately upset. In the desperate situation, I sent a cable
offering my temporary services to the Met. But the
Board declined, with thanks. They appointed Mr.

Gentele's assistant, Schuyler Chapin, on a temporary basis.

🔲🔲

When Goeran Gentele visited New York sometime in the late 1960s, he met Schuyler Chapin, then managing a summer festival of opera for Lincoln Center. The two gentlemen came to know and like each other. Chapin drew the attention of the Met's Board to Gentele. They, too, liked him. He was a very likable man. The Board eventually engaged him as my successor. Gentele, in turn, engaged Chapin as his assistant.

With Gentele's sudden death, the Board appointed Chapin on a temporary basis.

Chapin, an especially nice and pleasant gentleman, had no kind of opera experience. I am sure he had attended many performances of *Aïda, Tosca, Bohème,* etc., in his time. But it is a long way from knowing operas, to walking into the world's largest opera company saying, now I'll run it. He had no idea of the problems that would await him.

His temporary status was changed to that of the real General Manager in the hope that the improvement of his status would also improve the results. Apparently it did not work. The Company felt his lack of leadership.

After three years, a new formation came into

being. The Troika. It consisted of Anthony Bliss, James Levine and John Dexter.

I first met Anthony Bliss in 1949 in a corridor of the old Met when Edward Johnson, then General Manager, introduced us. I was surprised to find such a young man already a member of the Met Board. I did not know that Bliss's father had already been president of the Board.

Tony grew up with the Met atmosphere surrounding him. He took it very seriously, in contrast to some Board members who only considered it a social attribute. He took an enormous interest in the House, making a point of attending many performances. He got to know not only the glamorous stars but also the stagehands and wardrobe staff. He had as much knowledge as one could expect from an amateur which he was at that time.

Bliss and I really got on very well. Naturally there were occasional differences of opinion. But Bliss is a gentleman, and even arguments were always kept on a civilized level.

On one of the closing pages of my first book, the name of a very young conductor appears for the first time. During my next-to-last year at the Met, Ronald Wilford, President of Columbia Artists Management, the largest artists agency in the world, had drawn my attention to Mr. Levine, then totally unknown, a student of George Szell in Cleveland.

I flew out to hear him conduct, was most

impressed and engaged him at once for the Met, where he made his debut conducting *Tosca* on June 5, 1971, at the age of twenty-eight. He immediately became a leading conductor. There was no doubt from the first downbeat that here was an outstanding talent. Indeed today he has already made an international career with invitations from all over the world, including Salzburg, Vienna, Berlin and everywhere in the United States.

But *I* engaged him as a conductor, not as a Music Director, a position into which he was suddenly catapulted when he had hardly any experience in operatic administration.

In my time, there was no Music Director at the Met. I have said often and believe more and more that only ONE person must have the ultimate decision on any questions: financial, musical or dramatic. Needless to say, that person will and ought to take advice from his colleagues. I always did. But the final decision was mine.

The first Music Director Chapin appointed at the Met was Rafael Kubelik, a fine conductor and a nice man. He also was represented by Wilford. At that time Chapin did not grant Kubelik all the rights and prerogatives Wilford rightly wanted for his man. So even before the first season was over, Kubelik resigned. Thereafter Wilford obtained for Levine all he wanted. Levine's artistic rights were unchallenged.

To complete this management, John Dexter

was engaged. I had never heard his name but he was—and is—a talented British stage director who, I believe, had never set foot in an opera house, except perhaps as a spectator and that, I venture to guess, not too often. His position as Production Director had never really been defined.

I cannot say very much about Mr. Dexter. I have never met the man. His production of *Aïda* I found atrocious and very typical of a nonopera man. The soloists knew more or less what to do. But the chorus was hopeless. It seemed that the director had never worked with great masses. However, his staging of more contemporary works was very good.

Later there was an imported production from San Francisco of *Der Fliegende Holländer* which I considered an artistic impertinence. Rumor has it that nobody had taken the trouble to go to San Francisco to see this monstrosity before it was unveiled at the Met.

While I was hardly popular with the New York music critics, they did recognize the extraordinary talents of a team I was particularly proud of: Nat Merrill and Bob O'Hearn. They had remarkable success, one production after the other. Two pleasant young Americans, they were reliable and easy to deal with. Why have they never been asked back since I left? Indeed why has it taken ten years for Franco Zeffirelli, one of the great designers and directors of our day, to be asked back for a new production of *La Bohème?*

Naturally this management, like any, is responsible to the Board of Directors. A board is a very special animal and for the Metropolitan Opera, it is even more special. The directors of a bank or department store chain have to deal with business matters more or less equal to their own business. Certainly the question of expense and income is the same. But the problems in an opera house are totally different from anything they have ever heard of—the problems not of merchandise but of the result of human efforts, which cannot be measured in dollars and cents.

In my twenty-two years, I had to face a great many changes on my Board—sometimes for the better, sometimes for the worse.

Let me take George Moore as an example. He had no idea about opera, but he was intelligent enough to know it. One is not the head of one of the country's largest banks for nothing. I had a hell of a time with Moore, yet I respected his brilliant brain. Even on artistic matters, of which he admittedly had no knowledge, he would usually cut through the nonsense and deal with the heart of the matter. He had the courage to make decisions and stick to them. Even if they were wrong, one knew where one stood. The banes of the Board were usually those directors who "had taste" and, of course, money. They knew nothing of the real problems of the House except that there was a deficit. They felt, in some cases, that a genuine love for opera entitled them to decisions. If a director gives a few hundred thousand dollars, you have a hard time ignoring his views.

When talking about the Board, the first name that inevitably comes to mind is Mrs. August Belmont. In a way it is not easy to write about Mrs. Belmont. She died at the age of just over one hundred years. This, in itself, is remarkable—as the lady was. When I joined the Met she was already one of the most important, influential and distinguished members of the Board. She had been associated with the Met for more than fifty years.

With all her charm and kindness and her enormous intelligence, her fierce loyalty to the Metropolitan could result in her being bitingly sharp whenever she felt her beloved Company needed to be defended. I turned to her for advice on many occasions.

On my farewell broadcast, Mrs. Belmont was kind enough to say I was "a distinguished, re-markable man" and "we shall miss Rudolf Bing."

Mrs. Belmont's name will, and should, always remain linked to the Met. I am glad I had the privilege of knowing her.

THREE

W̲ITH THE M̲ET BEHIND
me, my thoughts were focused on my next assignment. When it became clear and public that I was
really leaving, all sorts of offers appeared. Among
the more interesting was one from John Lindsay,
then Mayor of New York.

John called sometime in the spring. "Rudi," he
said, "you cannot just retire. Why don't you join
Brooklyn College and pass some of your enormous
experience on to some young students who may
want to get into theatrical or operatic management?"

It seemed to make sense. John arranged for
me to meet the President and the Dean. They, in
turn, introduced me to the appointments committee. I had never taught. I really didn't know how
and what to teach. But I was gladly prepared to

share my experiences. So, having flunked every course in school, I got the job of "Distinguished Professor."

I was about to start a dialogue with young people on how theater works—artistically, technically and economically. I taught Music 20:30 and a seminar H801 on the managing of opera.

Teaching as such is not only an acquired technique but a natural talent. You either have it or you don't. I don't. As for the teaching, the title of "Distinguished Professor" notwithstanding, I found it was not my happiest experience. It was extremely difficult to plan a teaching program. I depended very much on the intelligence of my students.

You can learn driving or how to use machines, but management of theater depends on divergent people and talents. It can't be taught. You learn only by experience.

But the students always came. They were always there. I suspect the majority of them joined my classes because they had seen my name in the papers as "the man who fired Maria Callas." At least when they were asked by questionnaire about their reactions to me, one reported: "He's the best thing since the Beatles."

That same fall my first book, *5000 Nights at the Opera,* was published. I had promised the publisher to tour, promoting the book, on the days I wasn't involved at Brooklyn College.

The tour was another matter. Though quite exhausting, I found it gratifying to visit once again the many friends in the Met tour cities who have meant so much to all of us.

Cleveland, our first city, brought back many happy memories. I still remember, with fondness, the lovely party Mr. Strawbridge held for me in his offices at Higbee's Department Store.

Dallas was our second city, and I was delighted to be invited to the opening night of the opera season. I couldn't help but think of Maria Callas's statement when I fired her from the Met that art was produced in Dallas as opposed to the Met.

All I can remember was the generous hospitality at the several cocktail parties I was invited to in the huge lobby prior to the performance of *Dido and Aeneas* and *Pagliacci* with two Met luminaries: Raina Kabaivanska and Jon Vickers. I also remember my publisher's representative, Dick Boehm, walking up the aisle and somehow losing his trousers. In spite of that, over the years we became good friends—and still are.

The next morning I knew it was a different world. Dick and I arrived at a television studio at a somewhat unearthly hour. Dick appeared calm and tried his best to "serve" me but somehow I felt he was petrified that I would run from the studio never to be found again.

He introduced me to one of the other guests, Dale Evans, who said some very kind words. When she walked away I was totally bewildered. I had no idea who she was.

Dick informed me she was a popular star and the wife of Roy Rogers. I still recall the look on Dick's face when I asked: "Who is Roy Rogers?"

We met many more celebrities on this tour. I was introduced to Dana Andrews in a Minneapolis studio. Within seconds he rendered the Prologue from *Pagliacci*. Robert Merrill he wasn't. But he is a distinguished film actor who was touring on behalf of A.A. I was relieved that we met him in the morning for Dick's sake.

Having been a bookseller so many decades ago, I was amazed and delighted with what I saw on these trips. And I enjoyed being in Atlanta again, meeting Faith Bronson at Rich's and seeing one of the Met's best friends, and mine, Nancy McLarty.

Many weeks later we were in Philadelphia where I was autographing at Wanamaker's. There were so many guards surrounding me I felt as if I had been caught shoplifting. As elsewhere, there was a lovely reception. In this case the charming Mr. Reeves Wetherill held a private luncheon where I had the chance to talk, once again, with one of America's leading critics, Max de Schauensee.

Down "on the floor" I was informed that a modest, shy gentleman was waiting at the girdle counter. I asked Dick to find out who it was.

The "shy gentleman" turned out to be the great Rudolf Serkin, whose friendship goes back to when we were in school together over a half-century ago. We embraced and were happy to meet again, but I don't recall if he bought a book.

Some months after what I thought was the end of this promotion, I was asked to go to San Antonio to lecture during their annual spring festival. What began as a one-day visit became three, culminating in a performance of *La Traviata*. Beverly Sills was Violetta, a role I had never heard her sing before. It was a fine performance and, after her last curtain call, I went backstage to congratulate her.

Miss Sills describes this meeting in her highly entertaining book, *Bubbles*. She mentions an incident in her book that I would like to repeat in this. A young boy approached us, asking for our autographs. We both signed. I told him: "Young man, you are the only person alive who has both these signatures on one piece of paper."

As for the history of Beverly Sills versus Rudolf Bing, when I was at the Met, I simply did not care very much for her. For her somewhat off-the-beaten-track repertory, I had Sutherland and Caballé whom, quite frankly, I thought were better. There was nothing personal involved. In fact, at that time, I did not know Beverly. But I felt, in spite of public clamor, a manager has to have the courage of his convictions. When I left the Met, the very first thing my successor did was to offer a contract to her. It was his right and was the smart thing to do.

Sometime later I was running a series, *Artists Can Also Talk,* on radio station WQXR and very much wanted Beverly Sills. I was afraid that after my having kept her out of the Met for so long, she would not be willing to appear. She had every right to refuse to talk to me.

Well, I was wrong. I called her and she invited me to her apartment. She could not have been more friendly and graciously agreed to appear on the series. There was not an unpleasant word about the past. She was charming and showed her sense of humor. When I left, I felt we were friends.

Miss Sills has now given up her singing career and is General Director of the New York City Opera. I know that everybody wishes her well. She is a warm and honest person and, of course, knows the business from the ground up. I would not be surprised if the City Opera, under Beverly Sills, might create quite a few headaches for the Met.

My problems at Brooklyn College increased with each term. Every new group of students finally turned me into a record player. I soon found the situation intolerable.

Then, as it happened sometimes in my life, a

fluke changed the situation. Brooklyn College has a large concert hall that was, for the most part, unused. They asked me whether I would take over a sort of concert agency for their hall. I liked the idea—almost anything to get out of teaching. I thought out a little scheme. I would ask for an assistant in Brooklyn while I tried to find an office in Manhattan. Three days a week of traveling to Brooklyn was one thing. Six days was too much.

That decision led to one of my most important contacts, Ronald Wilford. I had lunch with him and asked if he would give me an office. He said he would if I would work for them. I asked what he wanted me to do. He answered, "We'll find something."

The very same evening he called me at home to tell me that his Board had unanimously approved my appointment as a Board member of Columbia Artists Management. I should come in the next day to meet my new colleagues and see my new office. It was too good to be true. The office is exactly four walking minutes from my home.

I hired Danny Banks who used to work for me at the Met. Now he was to report to me from Brooklyn while I handled most of my business from my new office.

As for Columbia, I could not have been received in a more friendly way. Of course I had known Ronald Wilford for years. He represented most good singers and even more conductors. We liked each other and worked well together during my years at the Met.

The only trouble was that it seemed to take a long time to find some work for me to do. I felt uncomfortable. All my life I had worked for my money, and here I got paid and frankly did almost nothing in return. I talked to Wilford, who could not have been nicer and generously assured me that my name on their Board added some prestige which he thought was worth the money. I did organize a concert series sponsored by Columbia and presented at Carnegie Hall. I really felt as I had fifty years ago in Vienna. I also made short speeches on behalf of Columbia at the conventions attended by music managements and the sponsoring organizations who book the artists and attractions around the country.

One of the divisions of Columbia is Community Concerts. It is a remarkable organization that functions in perhaps six to seven hundred cities where small committees are formed. Each employs a number of volunteers to enroll their friends and others to form a nucleus of an audience.

If they get groups of around one thousand people, a Community is formed and the head office will offer them a program. These are small towns as well as larger cities which could not hope to hear an Isaac Stern or a Domingo but which are interested in a group of three, four or more attractive concerts by young and lesser-known artists at very reasonable fees.

In this way, Community Concerts can offer some of their artists tours of twenty, thirty or more concerts to organized audiences that practically guarantee sold-out houses. Community has now run for many years under the brilliant leadership of George Blake and John Mazarella. The whole organization is an important wing of Columbia Artists Management.

For Community Concerts I formed a little touring company performing *Fledermaus*. Having produced it for the Met in my first year rather glamorously, I really ought to have been ashamed of this little touring company. Of course, no orchestra, but also no chorus and ballet. Well, how does one do Prince Orlofsky's party in the second act without chorus and ballet? For this company John Gutman rewrote Prince Orlofsky's song and, instead of champagne, he drank soda—a prince who had seen better days and was now broke.

We had two charming sopranos in Lou Ann Lee as Rosalinda and Christine Flasch as Adele. We also had two distinguished Met veterans. Theodor Uppman was Eisenstein and Frank Guarrera was Dr. Falke. And, of course, we played in small towns, most of whose population had perhaps never seen *Fledermaus*. At any rate they seemed to enjoy it. The houses were full and I was happy that the tour made a profit and so repaid some of my salary to Columbia.

In 1973, before this *Fledermaus* tour, I received a call from my former colleague Julius Rudel, then General Manager of the New York City Opera. He asked me whether I knew the opera *The Young Lord* by Henze, and I had to say I had never heard of it. He told me that the principal character of the opera was a silent part. Not a note to sing. Not a word to speak. It was a character, as Rudel told me, who should be distinguished-looking, elegant and arrogant. He thought I fitted the part perfectly. It was an amusing idea. I asked for a libretto. To my horror I found the character of the Young Lord hardly left the stage.

Sarah Caldwell was to direct and conduct the opera. Since I had always admired Miss Caldwell, I accepted. It turned out that it was she who suggested my name to Rudel, who also has a good sense of humor and accepted the idea.

I found the rehearsals quite strenuous. I learned that to be silent on a stage among others who sing is quite a disadvantage. You really have to dominate the stage with "personality," which is not easy. In fact, it is quite a physical strain and does not allow one a moment's repose. Never having been on a stage, I had the strange sensation of feeling almost physically elated when I had the audience's attention and also total emptiness when

I lost it. Miss Caldwell was a great help teaching me certain tricks and I am grateful to all my colleagues, especially my "nephew," Richard Fredricks.

Without doing anything, I seemed to help sell tickets. There was a certain curiosity as to how I would do. Somehow I got through it, but there has been no offer as yet to play Hamlet.

I received telegrams on opening night. One was from Birgit Nilsson which read: "Even if your role is speechless, I'm sure you will have the last word. Love, Birgit.

"P.S. Don't forget that many great artists have made their way from the City Opera to the Met."

FOUR

GETTING HOME FROM
SIUSI after nearly three months was always difficult, particularly for Nina who wanted everything
in the apartment orderly and would begin cleaning
before she had taken her coat off.

For me it used to be easy. I just went back to
the Met where my work was cut out for me. The
fall of 1972 was different. There was no more Met
to return to.

Nina was keenly aware of the drastic change
and tried to keep me busy at home when I wasn't
engaged in Brooklyn or on the book tour. We
rediscovered each other, going out for some din-
ners, which we had not done in years. We occasionally attended the theater or a movie and enjoyed it.
I really think Nina was glad to have me back. The

preceding twenty-two years of my life had really been centered at the Met. Nina had been alone a lot. Now we were together again.

⊒⊑

We were having a quiet dinner at home the evening of January 28, 1978, when suddenly and without a sound, Nina bent forward and slid from her chair.

I asked her to say something but she could not reply. With all my strength, I got her into an armchair and raced to the telephone to ask the hotel security men to come up and help get my wife to bed.

A few minutes later the Doctor arrived, and one look confirmed what I suspected. Nina had suffered a stroke. She was half-paralyzed and couldn't speak.

I did not immediately realize the magnitude of the disaster that had befallen us.

Very quickly an ambulance arrived and took us to Roosevelt Hospital where Nina was taken to intensive care. I was more or less dismissed.

It was a shattering experience after so short a time to come home to an empty apartment with the dishes of unfinished food still on the table. Eventually the place was in order and I went to bed.

It was horrible to face the empty bed next to

mine and my thoughts raced to the hospital, to my beloved Ninuschka. How would I find her the next morning?

She was alive and I thanked God for that. The only important change after four days was that she definitely recognized me and seemed to show some sign of pleasure when I visited her.

Some three weeks later the Doctor told me there was nothing more the hospital could do for her and that I should be looking for a nursing home. She would be cared for and I could visit. But this was the moment that counted in our lives, and I was determined not to leave her alone.

There was no acceptable nursing home in Manhattan that I knew of and, had I put her in one of those horror places, some floor nurse might have looked in every two hours or so. The rest of the time she would have been left alone except for my visits. Doctors and friends warned me of the mental perils of the situation for me, but I was adamant.

It is hard to explain the change that took place in my life. Outwardly it went on. I walked to the office in the morning. I made the daily visits to the hospital. But the desperation mounted. As the days went by I began to realize more clearly that *this was it.* Never again would Nina be able to talk. The lack of movement worried me less than her inability to speak. That was just devastating.

In a few weeks Nina came home. When the

door opened and she was wheeled in, I saw her relief to find herself home. It was *her* home with *her* pictures and *her* plants that she loves. There is no doubt that my awaiting her in the familiar sur- roundings lifted her spirits.

I was moved to tears when she motioned me to bring her the plants. She started picking little leaves here and there.

Now she needed nurses around the clock. That was possible only in that Columbia Artists Management has an excellent major medical insur- ance policy with the Equitable Life Assurance Society, which took care of us.

As the time went by, I learned to understand quite simple commands—if she wanted the blinds up or down it could be made clear with signs. Lights on or off could be understood. But if it went beyond these most simple requests I was helpless, which sometimes infuriated her. She thought she had asked a simple question and I just did not answer.

To this day, nobody including doctors can explain to me whether she knows she cannot speak. Nor can anybody advise me whether one should attempt to make it clear to her that she cannot be understood. It seems to me that aphasia is not really understood by the medical profession, and they know still less how to handle it.

I feel, however, that Nina does not suffer, and that is all that matters. Her eyes are calm. She bubbles along, and I find someway to answer her. I try to be home as much as possible and just sit by her side, trying to show her love. She watches television and sometimes laughs.

At times she shows slight displeasure when I go out for dinner but I simply cannot stay home every evening. I would go insane. So what seems a little selfish is really for her good. I must try to prevent my cracking up. I am all she has got and I must try to preserve myself. God knows it is not easy.

It is hard to accept that I will never again hear Nina, my beloved child who meant my life for over fifty years, speak a single word: "never again" became sort of a leitmotiv of my life.

Of course days vary from one to the other and I am afraid that, as time goes by, there are more and more bad days. The real problem is not to lose patience. All the time I have to say to myself, "Poor Nina. It is she who is sick and I have to help her." Sometimes it just doesn't work. I lose my temper, which usually has an immediate effect. But then I suffer more because I feel I have hurt her.

It is particularly difficult with any new nurse. Nina is terribly sensitive to new faces and so used to a certain routine that any slight deviation upsets her. As she cannot talk her only way to register protest is getting terribly upset and almost abusive toward the nurse.

We are so lucky with Mary Fahy, our chief

nurse, but she just has to have her days off and then trouble lurks. On such days I try to be home as much as possible. It does help Nina when I am around. On the whole I can improve matters but at a high cost to my nerves. I then go into the other room and cry, wondering how long I can take it.

Yet the idea that one day Nina may not be around anymore is even worse. I can almost feel the intense loneliness and above all the guilt feelings that will come up. The idea that I may go before her is almost too horrible to contemplate.

My doctor says that it is I who suffer more and that Nina has been reduced to a childlike simplicity, that she is not bored and quite content for the most part. It is true. Most of the time she sleeps well and eats well. Yet when I look into those calm but sad eyes I feel she is no longer in this world and I already miss her. Fifty years together with all the joys and, of course, some problems that fifty years naturally bring, is a lifetime together and cannot be broken.

Recently, I was invited to participate in the management of a new festival in Miami for 1982. I accepted and the next day asked to be out. Why? I just cannot face getting involved in some new work. I feel I am no longer able to do anything. Then I was persuaded to stay on—and did.

What is it? I complain of having little to do and, as soon as something appears, I want to withdraw. I no longer believe in my ability and am ashamed to live, as it were, on my name.

I cannot wait for the evening to go to bed. I spend as much time as I can with Nina, just sitting by her side and holding her hand. It is all I can do for her. But I know it makes her happy.

I feel guilty the few evenings I go out, returning home hardly ever much later than eight. I know she is waiting for me. It moves me to tears to see her happiness when I arrive.

I went to the opera one night and sat in the Bliss box, which used to be *my* box. I sat on my old chair in the back and thought of Nina sitting in front in one of her beautiful dresses, none of which she will ever wear again. During the intermission we all went to Tony's office, which used to be *my* office. Everybody was nice and friendly. I expect nobody noticed the pain it all caused me.

I did not stay for the dinner after the performance and raced home. Nina was asleep. I fell into my bed and cried myself asleep.

On a beautiful Sunday afternoon, I went out for a little walk by myself. Later I listened to the Philharmonic playing Tchaikovsky's Pathetic Symphony. Not exactly cheerful. Tonight I am home. The nurse very kindly cooks something for me. I really could not care less what it is. It is better than going out alone. I am certain it was the right thing to do to keep Nina at home instead of putting her in some nursing home as everybody suggested.

I know I ought to be grateful for so many things. I have no economic worries. I have a paid job at Columbia Artists Management. I live quite comfortably, and more important than anything else I can provide Nina with all the comfort and help she needs to make her unbearable life bearable. But I am desperately lonely.

Needless to say Nina's illness is the main cause of that. Also I never had too many friends. Some have died and others I feel shy of seeing too much. I know I am not good company these days. I don't want Nina to die. Yet I don't want to die before her.

So many dear ones are no longer here. I think of them often—with love and longing.

One of these dear friends died some years ago. Three days after her death, I received a letter from her, obviously written a few days before. I happened to mention this to a mutual friend. He suggested that if I received another letter from her to save the stamps.

The few friends left try to distract me. But my mind remains depressed.

🔲🔲

Some nights I lie awake and let my life pass through my mind. For over seventy years it was wonderful. I often think of my early days.

I look back about sixty-five years when we still lived in Vienna on Kaiser Josef Strasse. It was a beautiful old house with a wonderful wide staircase. The fact that there was no elevator did not seem to bother anybody even though we lived on the fourth floor.

The view was spectacular, looking across a huge square called Praterstern. We could see the Prater, the beautiful wide avenue with trees on both sides. It seemed endless. In the days when we still had a governess, which may go back another five or ten years, I was taken for a walk in the Prater nearly every day.

At the end of the Prater, which was a long walk from our house, we came to the "Lusthaus," an old chalet turned into a small and rather elegant little coffee house. No motor cars were allowed in the Prater. Indeed, in those days, there were not too many around. Only horse-drawn carriages.

On one side of the Prater, near where it began at the Praterstern, there was another avenue called "Wurstlprater," which was an amusement park with merry-go-rounds and trains going through dark tunnels where one saw all sorts of horrors. In fact, it was mainly used by young couples who wished to enjoy a few minutes of privacy.

My family spent many summers in "Aschau." You will not find it on any map. There used to be a tiny railroad which ran from Bad Ischl to Salzburg. The trip took about two hours. About twenty minutes from Bad Ischl, there was a stop, providing somebody waved or gave some sign to the conductor. This was Aschau, which consisted of two houses. These two houses were shared by our family and a family of friends. There was nothing but meadows and forests. It was wonderful.

School was not wonderful. I hated school. I made very few friends and brought home mostly bad marks.

In the morning my brother Ernst and I left home in time to catch the *Electrische*—a trolley. I remember one particular morning when my brother Robert was late and overtook us in a taxi while we stood, crammed in the *Electrische*.

Taking a taxi in those days was quite a daring feat and we admired Robert for it. I still don't know where he got the money.

When we grew older, my brothers were sent to Gmunden, a little town on a beautiful lake. There, an elderly lady, Fräulein Schwab, made her living by taking in boys from so-called "good" families to supervise and provide for them while they went to school.

I don't quite know why my parents chose Gmunden. I suspect school was a little easier there than in Vienna. They seemed quite happy and made good grades.

I was still too young to be sent away and also much too sensitive to have survived separation from my mother in those days.

For the holidays, my parents took me to Gmunden to visit my brothers, which was always fun and a happy time. In those days it took about five hours by train from Vienna. Today it probably is hardly more than two.

I was sent away around 1917 when school in Vienna just got too hard for me. I went to Baden, less than an hour away. Instead of Fräulein Schwab, Mr. and Mrs. Ehrmann were found for the boys who hoped to find school there a bit easier.

The trouble was that the Ehrmanns had a lovely daughter, Edith, who was just about my age. She did not encourage my schoolwork. Despite Edith, I felt terribly homesick. After a short time my mother, who shared my feelings, took me back to Vienna.

I stayed another year or two in school until my wise, good, understanding father took me out of school without my having passed a single examination. We discussed my future.

My mother sang very beautifully as an amateur. It was she who encouraged me in artistic endeavors rather than in commerce, which my brothers pursued, with some success.

Singing was always my great interest, and I studied quite seriously. In fact, there are not too many Schubert, Schumann, Wolf or Brahms lieder which to this day I don't know by heart. I tried to study singing with Franz Steiner, a good friend of Richard Strauss and undoubtedly the foremost interpreter of Strauss lieder. Soon I realized my voice was not big enough for a professional career.

The Steiners used to spend a good part of the summer with us. So it came that Richard Strauss, his wife and their son, Franz, also stayed at Aschau a good while. We all became friendly with the Strauss family.

One spring they invited my sister and me to stay with them in their lovely home in Garmisch, near Munich.

I remember all of us going to the opera in Munich to hear *Fledermaus*. When the magic music of the overture started, we were astonished to hear Frau Strauss turn to her husband—who was, after all, the greatest living composer—and tell him: "There, you see, Richard. *That* is music."

Strauss remained silent.

🔲🔲

I also studied painting for quite a while but my talents did not promise success on a professional basis in art either. We decided that I should enter the publishing field, which interested me and perhaps held some promise. Informed friends advised that bookselling was a good preparation for publishing. I took a job as a sales apprentice at Gilhofer and Ranschburg, an old and well-established Vienna bookshop. In the beginning I had to hold the large display windows while my older colleagues arranged the books.

I found out an interesting fact. The public doesn't always buy what they want. They buy what they see.

I read a lot at that time. Strangely enough I was most drawn to Russian literature. I say "strangely" because eventually I married a Russian. But in those earlier days I read almost all of Dostoievsky and Tolstoy as well as some of the other famous authors.

Of course it did not end with the Russians. I adored Hamsun and also read, with just a little less enthusiasm, Thomas Mann and some of the other famous German writers.

I was particularly interested in a book about Russia that was published at that time, the title of which I have now forgotten. I asked our book-buyer for copies. He said he would order three. I said I could not sell three copies but I could sell thirty. He thought he would try it. I filled a whole window with that book and sold them like the wind.

Soon after that I switched over to the concert agency, which was a department of the bookshop. That was really my start in music—or better in music management. In 1928 I was in Darmstadt under the director Carl Ebert. From there he took me with him to Berlin. Then I went to England and Glyndebourne, Edinburgh and eventually the Metropolitan Opera, where I later invited him as stage director. There I stayed until 1972, which seemed to have been a good career over the past fifty years.

As I look back to the early days in Vienna, many names go through my mind. I was on very friendly terms with the members of the Rosé Quartet, no doubt the foremost chamber music ensemble in those days, as well as with Rosé's daughter, Alma, a lovely girl.

There was hardly a week that I didn't spend at least one luncheon at their attractive little house in Döbling. Professor Rosé was rarely there because he and his quartet were continually on tours. But his wife, a charming lady and incidentally the sister of Gustav Mahler, was always there. And, of course, Alma, who was then around eighteen years old. Very naturally she studied the violin and, as her father thought, had reached quite a good level as an amateur.

Soon after Nina and I went to Glyndebourne, mother Rosé died. Alma came to England, where we saw much of her. Then, one day, she disclosed that she wanted to go to Holland to visit a friend. I tried to persuade her not to undertake this trip, but she went.

She was caught by the Nazis. Her story was portrayed in Arthur Miller's television drama *Playing for Time*, from which I gather that her violin kept her alive, leading the women's orchestra in Auschwitz until nearly the end of the war, when she died.

My relationship to the Hofmannsthal family goes back a long time. They had a lovely house in Rodaun, near Vienna. Christiane, Franz and Raimund—their daughter and sons—were good friends. In fact Christiane lives in New York and we are still in touch.

The older of the two sons, Franz, tragically committed suicide many, many years later. I don't think anybody really knew why.

Raimund was a man of great charm. I was very fond of him. Just a few years younger than I, he died not too long ago. It was a great personal loss to me.

Gertie, the mother, was a charming lady and I am proud that even Herr Von Hofmannsthal, one of the great poets of our time, tolerated me occasionally on my frequent visits to their house.

There were quite a few summers when we all met in Alt-Aussee. Christiane and I made many excursions together.

The whole family represented the best that Vienna of those days had to offer.

I knew most of the singers at the Vienna Opera and worked for Alfred Piccaver, the famous and wonderful tenor. To this day I have not heard anyone like him. And there were Maria Olczewska, Sigrid Onegin, Hans Duhan and many others.

I was present at many a performance at the Vienna Opera. One I particularly remember was Maria Jeritza's first performance after her return from her first American visit. The Viennese were jealous of "their" Jeritza. When she appeared as Elisabeth in *Tannhäuser* with the famous entrance *"Dich, teure Halle, Gruess ich wieder,"* the house came down.

I remember *Lohengrin* with Aagaard Oestvig, the very good-looking Scandinavian tenor—the best Lohengrin I have ever heard—along with Lotte Lehmann, Paul Schoeffler and Richard Mayr. This was considered an "ordinary" performance. No special prices. No special publicity.

Tosca with Jeritza, Piccaver and Schoeffler was again a "regular" performance. Today, this sort of cast would take the performance out of the subscription with vastly increased prices and special publicity. And there are no singers around who could compare. Other singers, almost as good, were the "ensemble." It was only years later that singers traveled for long periods of guest performances. Of course, there was no flying in those days.

Strangely enough, as I look back now, not too much attention was paid to the conductor. Was it perhaps because they were all so good?

But that is not really true. Of course Franz Schalk, who also served as the director of the House, was a superb conductor. And so was Clemens Krauss, among others. And there was, of course, Richard Strauss who conducted not only his own works but others as well.

Today I do attend a few concerts that give me much pleasure. While writing this book I went to the Metropolitan Museum to hear Hermann Prey sing *Die Winterreise*. It was a beautiful evening.

Winterreise is particularly close to my heart. I remember singing it at home in Vienna more than fifty years ago. My brother Robert accompanied me at the piano—atrociously.

FIVE

M

ARIA CALLAS WAS
the superstar of stars. She not only had a glorious
voice, she was musical and had an enormous stage
personality and good looks. There was nothing
missing.

She needed no advice from any manager. She
knew what parts to sing and what parts to avoid.
She knew what fees to ask for and what to refuse. I
feel that Callas and nobody else established opera
in Chicago. I don't want to minimize the excellent
work of Miss Carol Fox and Mr. Lawrence Kelly in
the early years, but it was Callas who decided what
she wanted to sing, and it was her personal success
that made opera possible in Chicago.

It was fascinating to watch Callas work with a
stage director. She knew after five minutes

whether he was any good or not. If she worked with a man like Zeffirelli she cooperated to the utmost. If the director was uninteresting, she would just ignore him and do what she wanted—and usually it was good and exciting. She knew the effect she wanted to produce—and did. Callas would not shy away from an ugly tone if it would produce the desired dramatic effect.

As the world knows, I did not always get along with Maria. It was during one of those periods we were not on good terms that I visited Milan for the first time. There was no performance at La Scala, only a stage rehearsal.

Visiting the General Manager, Signor Ghiringelli, in his office, I told him that even though there was no performance that evening, I would love to see the House.

The small difficulty was that it was Callas rehearsing.

Signor Ghiringelli said he would let me in if I went to the gallery. If Callas spotted me in the House, she would walk out.

Fortunately, not much later we made up again and were really good friends for most of the time.

Alas, she did not keep her voice long. Her end was tragic and, although I have nothing to support my view, I felt that she, herself, ended her life. It may well have been unbearable to sink from the top of the world to her total loneliness in Paris.

At the end, before she withdrew from her

world to her apartment, she attempted a last concert tour. Her concerts in the West including Carnegie Hall were disasters, while strangely enough in Japan she enjoyed great success. Asked how to explain this, I could only say that tastes differ. The Japanese also like raw fish.

Needless to say, I was always anxious to get Callas back to the Met. Unbeknownst to the public, Maria and I communicated not long after I fired her in 1958. I remember in late 1959 picking up the telephone and finding Maria at the other end. We had a perfectly friendly conversation. I followed the call with this letter.

Dear Maria:

I am delighted that you seem to feel, as I do, that in spite of disagreements and difficulties, our personal relationship is such that we can freely and frankly communicate with each other.

To the important question of the future. My dear Maria, you must know from our past negotiations that I am planning my seasons usually eighteen months ahead of time. That means to say the outline of a season's repertoire is set in June of the previous year and by the time one season opens, at the end of October or November, the next season is usually pretty far advanced in planning. At this stage, that is to say at the middle of December, next season is completely set, down to rehearsal schedules and, of course, principal castings. The great majority, indeed nearly all, of the important contracts are signed. Consequently there is absolutely nothing "interesting" that I could offer you and to be quite frank there is hardly anything in the repertoire that I could offer you. We are not even planning *Tosca, Traviata* or *Lucia,* all of which are supposed to have a year's rest.

However, naturally I want you back and, if you feel that you would like to reappear in New York just to show yourself to your many New York friends, I would certainly be very willing to make an effort. Now please don't shoot at me but I think I could, shortly before Christmas with one rehearsal, revive *Traviata.* I know our production is not exactly a favorite of yours but there it is. It seems to me one of the very few works which has been played so often in recent years that we could revive it in a minimum of time which could be made available. So we could probably find two or three *Traviata* performances. I am well aware that this does not sound very attractive or very tempting. It is merely to show you that even at this much-too-late moment I would like to make possible your return, at least just to show that you have not forgotten New Yorkers and to show you that they no doubt have not forgotten you.

Honestly, this is about all I can see at the moment. Please let me just have a short line, but if possible by return because even that now takes considerable rearrangement, whether some such arrangement would interest you. If not, we will have to wait for another year. If it does interest you, I will then as quickly as possible make more detailed suggestions.

I received a letter from Maria. Among other things, she said she was happy that this time the press changed my words and not hers. She felt that the press always tried to mix things up.

She continued that she was sorry that at the moment I had no other really interesting work for her—some new revival that would make news.

Anyway, she finished the letter asking me to let her know as soon as something interesting came up.

And again I wrote. And again Maria replied that she would like to come back to the Met. But that it will depend on me. She was willing to listen if the ideas were good. She then stated she might consider a *Tosca* for Mrs. William Randolph Hearst's Milk Fund Benefit if she could have Corelli and a good baritone.

I was pleased that she told me of her great friendship and her pleasure to hear from me. The feeling was mutual.

Dear Maria:

It was nice hearing from you again.

Surely you know that our planning is always much further ahead than just for a few weeks, so, delightful as it sounds, I could not possibly invite you for this season; not only is *Tosca* not in this season's repertory but Mrs. Hearst's benefit performance on March 23rd has long been settled and we are now in our 16th week of the season, so there really are only 9 weeks left: I am afraid, and I am sure you will understand, there is nothing I can do right now.

Indeed, plans for next season have been completed but next season there will be *Tosca* and *Traviata* in the repertory and, while all performances have already been scheduled, if you really want to come back I would be delighted to put on an extra special Sunday performance for you and suggest either

Traviata on November 5 or *Tosca* on November 12, 1961. Needless to say, I would be extremely happy to welcome you back to the Metropolitan. Let me know whether this suggestion in any way appeals to you.

Kind regards

She did return in *Tosca* in 1965. Though she may not have been in her top form, the audience was just delirious.

Then I had what I thought was a really good idea: The *Josephslegende*—a mime by Hofmannsthal with music by Richard Strauss. Of course I had to give her an explanation, as she was too young to have heard of the sensation the work had caused at the Vienna Opera many years before. In a few words, it was the story of Potiphar trying to seduce Joseph. To Strauss's exciting music Hofmannsthal wrote not a ballet, but a mime, with Potiphar the central figure—without speaking or singing a word. In my early days, as a growing boy in Vienna, Marie Gutheil-Schoder acted Potiphar; she was in her time one of the leading singers of the opera—somewhere approaching Jeritza in singing and acting. She was a sensation and I was convinced Callas would also be.

101

New York
December 12, 1967

CONFIDENTIAL

Dear Maria,

I have at last obtained an English version
of "The Legend of Joseph" by Hofmannsthal
and music by Richard Strauss and I also have a
piano score with English descriptions. They
are rare copies which I obtained with difficulty
from Boosey and Hawkes and I would be most
grateful if you would take good care of these
two things and in due course return them to
me.

I don't think this is the moment to go into
any further details. I just want you to read it
and to let me know whether you are interested. I would then take it from there. I would
not contemplate the whole thing without you,
but if you are interested, which would delight
me, then we can discuss the matter further as
to period and in particular also what to do
preceding the *Legend*—I think it plays a little
less than one hour.

If you are interested, I might come to
Paris to discuss the matter further with you
unless, which would be more helpful, you

might be prepared to fly over here and talk things over with us. I mentioned it to Jean-Louis Barrault just in passing and I think if we can agree on the time he would be fascinated to work with you, while I would get a choreographer for the rest of the show. Think it over. Please keep it strictly confidential and let me hear from you as soon as you can.

Yours sincerely,

Rudolf Bing

Maria answered a few weeks later that she had carefully examined the score and libretto. She found the project fascinating although she wanted it combined with another role which she could sing. Otherwise she feared people would draw unfavorable conclusions.

She again ended with expressions of friendship and emphasized how much she enjoyed her visit to the new Met.

New York
January 31, 1968

CONFIDENTIAL

Dear Maria,

Thank you for your letter. I am delighted that you seem interested in the idea.

Of course I would love you to sing at the Metropolitan again. If you say, "It would have to be together with something to sing," do you mean something to sing at the same evening or an opera in the repertory?

If you meant something to sing at the same evening, there is another wonderful idea which I put to you. Do you know Cocteau's play *La Voix Humaine* with music by Poulenc? It is a one-act opera for one solo voice: a woman who is on the telephone to her lover and in the end kills herself. It is a phenomenal acting part and I could not think of anyone better for it than you. It must be very easy for you in Paris to get a score, but please be very careful—I am terribly anxious to keep this whole matter really confidential and eventually, hopefully, announce it as the sensation it would be, rather than let some silly gossip journalists get hold of it.

Now the next step is for me to wait until I hear from you about the Poulenc piece. It would still be a very short evening, but I think to get Callas twice, once perhaps with Nureyev, is enough for one evening, even if it is not too long. If we start five minutes past eight with the Poulenc, then one can easily have a thirty- or forty-minute break which if you don't need it, the public will need it to recover, and then *Joseph's Legend* will take it to a little after 10 o'clock. I think that would be enough.

If you don't like the idea about *La Voix Humaine* then we would have to find something else to go with *Joseph's Legend*—possibly another ballet or some orchestra pieces, but that would be less easy to find and then we would have to look for something else in the season concerned that interests you.

One of my problems, which I am considering now, is whether this should go into the subscription ... perhaps twelve or fifteen performances in six or seven weeks (plus preceding rehearsals), or whether we should do it sometime in the summer for a few weeks every night, seven times a week—or does that idea shock you?

I have not yet approached Nureyev, because I don't want him to talk about it until you and I are clearer about how we really want to proceed, so may I have your thoughts on

the matter when you will have read this letter?
Kindest regards.

Yours sincerely,

Rudolf Bing

Then a letter came from her declining my
suggestion of *Joseph's Legend.*

February 27, 1968

Dear Maria,

I have your letter of the seventh of February and am very sorry and very disappointed.
I thought you had liked the idea and I still
think your appearance as Potiphar would have
been a sensation and I suppose also pretty
lucrative.

I never quite understood whether you
wanted to sing at the same evening (the *Joseph
Legend* is not a full evening) and only in that
case did I suggest *La Voix Humaine.* If you want
to do a regular opera on other evenings—
preceding or succeeding a possible season of
the *Joseph Legend,* I am, of course, open to

suggestions. Would you care to do *Medea* if we can borrow the Dallas production or what else would interest you? Do let me hear from you again.

Have you been good enough to return the score and the German libretto to me? I have faithfully promised Boosey and Hawkes to return it to them and I would be grateful to hear whether you have sent it—it has not yet arrived.

Kindest regards and best wishes.

Yours sincerely,

Rudolf Bing

Then I wrote to her if she would do *Lucia,* which she also declined. She asked for another opera "less perilous." She said she was in Paris and expected to hear from me again.

SORRY ABOUT LUCIA WILL ATTEMPT SUBSTITUTE BUT PLEASE MAKE SOME SUGGESTIONS WOULD YOU ACCEPT MEDEA IF CAN ARRANGE WITH DALLAS OR PERHAPS TRAVIATA WHAT ELSE REGARDS BING

She cabled back that she would accept *Medea* if she could have an excellent cast for all performances.

Office Memorandum
METROPOLITAN OPERA

TO Robert Herman

FROM R.B.

Siusi   DATE June 21st 68

Dear Bob, just sent you a cable, that Maria "would like *Medea* provided excellent cast for all performances." I simply don't remember the cast well enough—is George Schick around to advise? I would not necessarily tell Kelly that it is for Maria, though if he asks you cannot swindle him. Could Gedda do the tenor part? Why not ask Nikki—it might interest him; I seem to remember that Vickers did it?? Would he be available—but Gedda would be better, because we have him for the period, I think.

Conductor: Is there any chance for Giulini—now that he is there? Or should we go for Franci, whom I had offered *Lucia,* which he accepted. By the time you get this he may have had his debut—what reaction? Director:

Would Nat Merrill be available? Who did it in Dallas—when was that?

I very much hope we can bring that off—it would add enormous glamour to the season—as many performances as you like: 7 or 8. Let me hear as soon as you have something to report.

Just had a cable from Herman Krawitz—apparently you all will have to suffer me for another four years . . . well, we shall see; tell Herman if he has any confidential news about what went on during the meetings naturally I would be interested.

Kind regards.

Siusi, June 23rd 68

Dear Maria,

Since your cable I have been twice in touch with N.Y. and I am afraid this season it may not work with *Medea*. The point is that for *Lucia* we had allowed (in addition to some time on the rehearsal stage) five days on stage; that for *Lucia* would have been quite enough: the orchestra knows it the chorus knows it, everybody knows the production, which is quite new, so one day lighting, two days with piano and one day with orchestra plus a dress rehearsal would have been all right—it would also be enough for *Traviata,* which was a new production in the new House, done last year and this past season—but not for *Medea,* which is totally new for everybody—orchestra, chorus and everybody else don't only not know the production, they don't even know the work. So in addition to considerably more time for musical preparation and rehearsal stage work, we would need at least 8 or 9 days on stage—and this seems a minimum—possibly even more. Even if we get Dallas to loan us the sets, it would still be a new production for us, for which we rarely have less than 12 to 14 days on the actual stage. However, with this coming season completely prepared, subscriptions as well as all engagements, we simply cannot make more than these five days available at this late stage. Bob Herman is once again looking in to it very carefully, but from my last talk with him, I cannot be very hopeful for this season. You have no answer about *Traviata*—this we might be able to do—would you let me know; failing that, I would hope for *Medea* next season and will be in touch with you about it soon after my return mid-August.

If you can still see your way to accepting *Lucia* or *Traviata*—please send me another cable, which would make me very happy. It was lovely seeing you again,

September 30, 1968

Dearest Maria:

I was distressed that our meeting first in Paris and then in New York fell through; with all the great difficulties involved I had hoped that in personal conversation we might have reached a satisfactory conclusion. I fear it may be even more difficult with time-consuming correspondence. From what you told me on the telephone I take it that there really is no hope for the season 1969/70 if all your commitments, as you described them to me, are final and unchangeable.

As I told you, we would have to replace a work which has been scheduled in our repertory and for which artists have been engaged in order to accommodate *Medea*, but another three or four weeks have gone by and the switching around of artists does not get easier. Furthermore, I read the other day that you may be doing *Medea* not only in Dallas and San Francisco but also with the Dallas Company in New York at the old City Center on 55th Street. I can really hardly believe that, but nevertheless I have to ask you about it because that would obviously make it quite unnecessary for us even to think about the change in next year's program.

I don't know whether you have ever been in the old City Center on 55th Street. It seems incredible to me that you should have accepted to appear there, but of course I don't know. In general, your return to New York with another Company is nothing that can particularly delight the Metropolitan Opera, as you will readily understand. Even apart from your *Tosca* appearances in the old house I have tried for years to get you back and I would like to try again if you give me a reasonable chance. May I hear from you again?

Kindest regards.

Yours ever,

Rudolf Bing

On the same day, I received another "Dear Rudolf" letter. She explained she was exhausted when I was in Paris and had to leave the same evening we were to meet.

She related she had heard from George Moore about my nagging that she gave up our three scheduled rendezvous, reminding me that there were actually two.

What distressed me was her comment that I

actually wasn't making things possible for her return to the Met as she felt she should. She asked me to try a little harder. I thought I had.

I immediately wrote to George Moore.

October 3, 1968

Mr. George Moore

Dear George:

The enclosed was received today from Maria. What am I to do with the dame? My fear is that she just wants me on my knees begging her to come, making all arrangements—and then she will cancel. I really am not terribly keen, life is difficult enough. What do you think?

You will note that my letter to her of the thirtieth, of which I sent you a copy, apparently crossed with hers.

Kind regards.

Sincerely,

Rudolf Bing

New York
May 5, 1969

Dear Maria,

Again, it is ages that we have not heard from each other. I wish I knew how you are, indeed, where you are and what your plans are.

Today I want to come back to a plan I suggested to you sometime in 1967. I then, in December of that year, sent you an English version of *Joseph's Legend* and I had a letter from you in January 1968 in which you told me you were fascinated "by the score and the libretto," but at that time, for various reasons, did not feel that you wanted to proceed. I again wrote to you in January and February of 1968, and that is where the matter so far rested.

It has now become very much alive again by the considerable interest . . . Mr. Sol Hurok has shown in the project. I talked to Mr. Hurok about it today and he was enthusiastic. Obviously Hurok, much more than I, is the man to put the thing on if anybody can put it on, and Hurok shares my view that with you this could not only be a world sensation but also a matter of considerable artistic and economic interest for yourself.

Hurok is willing to come to Paris immediately to discuss it with you and, indeed, if you would still be interested and would consider a premiere approximately a year from now at the Metropolitan Opera House, plans would have to be formulated right away.

May I ask you to be good enough to send me a cable when and where you might be willing to see Mr. Hurok?

Kindest regards.

Yours ever,

Rudolf Bing

cc: Mr. Sol Hurok

May 5, 1969

PERSONAL AND CONFIDENTIAL

Dear Mr. Hurok:

Please find enclosed copy of my letter to Maria Callas together with copies of all the letters that have so far been exchanged in the matter with her and also copy of a letter to Boosey and Hawkes which gives you some of the details of what is available. Needless to say if and when I hear from Mme. Callas I will immediately be in touch with you but until then I take it you will treat the matter as very confidential.

Kind regards.

Yours sincerely,

Rudolf Bing

Then came another letter finally declining *Joseph's Legend.* She advised me that she was free in the autumn and hoped to hear from me. She sent regards to Mr. Hurok, to my wife and to me.

May 19, 1969

Dear Maria:

I am very disappointed about your declining the *Joseph Legend.*

There is not too much time left for your re-entry at the Metropolitan if you want to do it as long as I am still here. I am trying to get out. I have had twenty years of it now and really feel I have not deserved more.

116

I had hoped that the *Joseph Legend* would be a sensational re-entry, which in turn would clear the way for anything else you might wish to do.

Why don't you go to Dallas, which was announced all over the place?

Do let me hear from you again. I will be leaving at the end of this week for two weeks' vacation in the Dolomites (Pensione Mirabella, Bolzano, Siusi), but alas, back here on June 9th for union negotiations.

Kindest regards.

Yours ever.

As the world knows, Maria Callas did not return to the Met or to any other opera house.

She dazzled the world like a diamond but she did not warm us like Renata Tebaldi. In some ways they were almost opposites.

No doubt these sopranos were the reigning rivals in the fifties. There were those who would consider Tebaldi's voice superior. Indeed in the top register, Tebaldi had a warmth and roundness of sound Callas missed. Yet, perhaps it was just the cozy warmth that made Tebaldi miss the unique Callas personality. To Tebaldi purity of tone was all important. She had the more beautiful voice. While Callas could hold the audience with the move of an arm, Tebaldi could ravish the house

with the beauty of tone. Tebaldi suddenly withdrew and is no more heard from.

There were singers one thought would make
world careers who simply vanished from the scene;
others, whom one did not think too much of,
suddenly rose to stardom and overshadowed their
colleagues.

There were, of course, those for whom it was
not difficult to predict the future. But there are
artists who in spite of great qualities have not
ignited the public's imagination. One such artist
was Lucine Amara.

When she sang in the opening night of my first
season at the Met as the offstage "celestial voice," I
really thought she was at the start of a great career.
She sang exquisitely. She soon was promoted to
leading roles and sang every season during my
administration.

Yet, somehow she did not make it. Everybody
liked her. Everybody acknowledged the beauty of
her voice. She was pleasant to look at. But somehow she did not excite the public to the extent of,
say, Callas, Milanov or Tebaldi.

While I cannot pretend to have been close to
the artists I engaged, I did enjoy a few friendships.

Leontyne Price is not only a superb singer, in a
class by herself, but in addition is a warm and
helpful person. Indeed that is not always the case
with artists. I am proud to call her a friend.

Leonie Rysanek is not only a wonderful singer

but also a loyal member of the Met. And luckily, she too, in addition to being a superb artist, is a friend whom I treasure.

Grace Bumbry seems to me the leading mezzo; she has only recently and most successfully changed into the soprano repertory. While she is surely a loss to the mezzos, she is a serious artist with no nonsense about her.

Turning to the men, we start naturally, with the king of the beasts—the tenor. It is not hard to pick Placido Domingo and Luciano Pavarotti. Both are head and shoulders above their competitors. Obviously people will have their favorites. I would like to stay out of that race. They are both quite exceptional tenors, and the Met is lucky to have them at the same time. From what I hear, neither of them seems to be difficult to handle.

Oh, where is Corelli???

Hardly anybody doubted his world career and success. And indeed, he had it. In my view he is the greatest tenor of his day. He is also a warm-hearted human being.

Sherrill Milnes has a tough job. He really is expected to replace Warren and Merrill. I think Milnes fills this difficult spot admirably. His voice is just strong enough for the Italian heroic parts and also has the sweetness and legato for the more lyric roles.

Jerome Hines, who made his debut before my time, in 1947, is one of the outstanding basses at the Met, and at the time of this writing is still singing impressively. His Grand Inquisitor in *Don Carlo* is hard to beat. He is also the longest reigning leading singer at the Met, breaking the long-time record of Antonio Scotti.

Cesare Siepi is a noble bass of international distinction whom I was proud to introduce to the Met. He stayed there all through my time and indeed was acknowledged and hailed as the great artist he is.

Not long after Leontyne Price's spectacular debut at the Met, we were fortunate to have another distinguished black soprano, Martina Arroyo. One day, Arroyo was entering the stage door when she was greeted as Miss Price. Her reply was: "I'm the other one, honey."

Today, I am happy to say the Met has the services of many excellent black artists. I was happy that Marian Anderson was the first black singer I could introduce to the Met. (Actually the first black artist who set foot on the Met stage was Janet Collins, a superb dancer.)

Yes—there was some opposition. But the great contralto and I just ignored it. Today black artists appear at the Met and nobody lifts an eyebrow. That is as it should be.

I looked for voices—not colors.

I often thought, no matter how difficult their jobs are, the President of the United States and the

Mayor of New York don't have to deal with prima donnas. No matter how well you get along with most, if you have no problems with ninety-eight and tiffs with two others, the press will report on the two.

But what would the Met do without them? And what would the Met do without those artists who have an enormous repertory and who are available to cover? Naturally you can't expect an artist to cover and not be given performances. While the public might have preferred another singer, I was grateful that we had artists of such high caliber.

From time to time we had problems with our standing room audience. One problem involved one of our most important singers. I wrote (in part):

> I am trying to get at the bottom of incidents which, as you know, have led to press statements, both of which were as unpleasant to you as they were to the management, in regard to your so-called "claque."
>
> Nobody complains about "prolonged ovations" which, fortunately, quite a few of our artists receive. The only complaint is about

hostile demonstrations against another artist and, in general, unruly behavior. I would clamp down on this irrespective of whose claque or fans were involved. If you are suggesting that there are certain factions try- ing to discredit you, this may be true and this is just one of the reasons I have attempted to find out the truth. You have no justification whatever to say that these "claques" have been successful in their efforts, because you have again no justification to say that the manage- ment has in any way expressed suspicion of your own behavior or your own involvement in this whole affair. You must be as interested as I am in clearing up what is an unhealthy and unfortunate situation and my efforts to do so should find your support and not your criticism.

I am delighted to hear that your con- science is clear and in fact I have had no doubt about this. I am fully aware that you are giving of your best and you have plenty of justifica- tion for assuming that I gratefully acknowl- edge these efforts. Let us hope that the next season will find things calmer and on a more dignified level.

I look forward to seeing you on tour and am, with kind regards,

When I talked to the Columbia University

undergraduate school many years ago, some of the students disclosed that there were frequent standing room visitors who suffered what they called considerable harassment, which contrasted greatly to their treatment at the State Theater.

At the State Theater their tickets were checked when they came in, and that was the end of it, while at the Met, they told me, they had to show their ticket stubs five or six times in the course of an evening. They were, as they put it, "herded in" and apparently treated rather roughly; they felt demeaned.

I didn't know the reasons for this treatment and what appeared to me somewhat too strict discipline. I felt we ought to rethink our attitude toward standing room patrons and, in general, to students and young patrons. We wanted to encourage them and not discourage them. Frankly, if, during the last act of an opera, somebody sneaked in and took an empty seat, I did not consider that to be a crime, as long as the ushers did not accept money for it.

And yet the claques continued to be a nuisance. I wrote to our leading artists:

> Despite the Management's continued efforts to do away with the claque in this theater this regrettable institution has by no means disappeared, and in fact it would seem that in recent weeks it has shown up with

particular virulence. The Management has received an ever-increasing number of letters by subscribers who complain—and quite rightly—about this unbearable nuisance.

Nothing is, of course, more desirable in an opera house than applause and enthusiasm in general. Both artists and Management would certainly rue the day, if it ever came, when there would be silence after a great aria or at the end of an act. However, it seems to me, and I do think that it should appear to all real artists, that paid applause is a reflection on rather than a sign of artistic merit.

Approximately a year ago the Management approached all solo artists with a request to refrain from using any claque, and solo artists at that time agreed to this. Unfortunately it is now quite clear that some of those artists have either not kept their promises or else have in the meantime decided to return to the claque system.

This letter is addressed to all solo singers, and the fact that it is sent to you in no way implies that you necessarily are one of the offenders in this case. However, in any case, the Management would once again like to ask you earnestly to help us in another effort to stamp out this bad custom. While we have no intention whatever of putting a stop to any kind of legitimate approval of our singers' fine performances, we will no longer tolerate the abuse that recently has been noticed and in fact will employ any means within our power to protect the civilized members of our audiences against being disturbed by those who would seem to confuse an opera house with a circus.

The sole purpose of this letter is to ask you once again for your assistance and to express the hope that our joint efforts in this direction will succeed in bringing back to the Metropolitan that dignity of which it has always been justifiedly proud and which in recent weeks has been so regrettably lacking.

But claques were not the only problems I had with artists. To an important artist about to make a Met debut, I wrote:

I am terribly upset at the unexpected difficulties that are suddenly arising. It seems that our friend Roberto Bauer was unsuccessful in explaining to you the basic differences in the Metropolitan's repertory system as against the Scala's *stagione* system. I cannot attempt to explain it all in a letter and I look forward to an early opportunity of discussing all these problems with you when you are here. In the meantime, you must forgive me if I try to analyze the situation clearly and factually.

You have signed a contract with us quite a long time ago, a contract in which we have undertaken to give you an exceedingly high guarantee of performances and you have undertaken to sing certain parts. One of these parts—all of which has been carefully discussed with you and negotiated over a long period prior to your signing—was Des Grieux in *Manon Lescaut*. You have now eliminated that part from the agreed repertoire and, while this caused difficulties for us, we have accepted it without protest.

Then you said you would not sing another role. This caused enormous difficulties both in New York and, indeed, insuperable difficulties on the tour. You cannot be aware of all the serious problems these sort of sudden changes cause. Our organization is not run like the Scala and cannot be run like the Scala. However, again, in order to meet your requests we have rearranged the schedule.

I am looking forward to your coming—so are we all, and so is the New York public. I will advise you to the very best of my ability and I think you should trust me. I have now many years of experience at the Metropolitan and have not been too unsuccessful in building various artists' careers here.

While most artists took their engagements seriously, a few would gladly relinquish a Met performance for a more lucrative engagement. I wrote to one:

I am sure you will permit me to say that I don't consider it fair that because of the great money that accrues to you from your work away from the Met you want the Metropolitan Opera to give up a performance here. This seems to me a totally wrong approach. Your Metropolitan public would feel greatly upset if they learned that you just gave up a Metropolitan performance so that you can make some more money in a resort hotel. I don't think it is fair and, in fact, I don't think it is fair that you should ask me, because every time you ask me for something which I cannot grant, you are then upset and create an embarrassing and unpleasant situation which I regret.

And once a singer wrote to me:

My dear Mr. Bing,

I would just like to tell you, and I do mean to tell you, that I will do the high E-flat at the end of the first act of *Traviata* on Saturday. I also intend doing it in all of my performances from now on.

I know you have what you think are valid reasons for not wanting this, but I, unfortunately, am more convinced than ever that I can no longer present my Violetta to the Metropolitan audience and above all to our great radio public differently as I do it *[sic]* in every other concert or operatic presentation other than the Met all over the world.

I feel sure that you will understand this decision, which is very final I assure you.

If you cannot bring yourself to agree with me on this very minor difference this time, then I guess you will have to find another soprano.

Please understand that this is a very serious artistic point on my part and not just another ham singer's whim for a mere vocal effect.

Needless to say, the high E flat brought down the house. But so did other moments far less spectacular. In one well-publicized season I wrote to our principal artists:

I have given careful consideration to the problem of curtain calls after scenes, acts and

My mother on her wedding day.

My father.

Nina in her dancing days in Vienna.

A rehearsal of *Don Carlo* before my first opening night at the Met. From left to right: Delia Rigal, Cesare Siepi, Margaret Webster and Robert Merrill. Jussi Bjoerling has his back to us. To the right: Garson Kanin, Fritz Stiedry and the new General Manager. *Below*, Congratulating Roberta Peters after her successful debut as Zerlina in *Don Giovanni*. To her right is Max Rudolf. (*credits: Sedge LeBlang*)

Maria Jeritza returns to the Met after a long absence in my first season, as a special request from me for a performance as Rosalinda in *Fledermaus*. (*credit: Sedge LeBlang*)

Standing between Eleanor Steber and Patrice Munsel during an intermission of *Fledermaus*. (*credit: Metropolitan Opera Archives*); Below, Surveying the empty stage at the old Mct. (*credit: Sedge LeBlang*)

Walking Pip. (*credit: Metropolitan Opera Archives*)

With Milton Cross, Risë Stevens and Richard Tucker. (*credit: Metropolitan Opera Archives*)

Mrs. Arthur Hays Sulzberger, Dag Hammarskjold (partially hidden), my sister Ilka, Sir Pierson Dixon, Mr. Arthur Hays Sulzberger and Lady Dixon join Nina and myself at the old Met. (*credit: Sedge LeBlang*)

Paul Schoeffler as the Grand Inquisitor and Jerome Hines as King Philip in *Don Carlo*. (*credit: Louis Melançon*); *Left*, Jerome Hines as the Grand Inquisitor. (*credit: Sedge LeBlang*)

at the end of performances and have come to the conclusion that the Metropolitan Opera should follow the example of La Scala in Milan and the Vienna State Opera—no doubt the two leading opera houses in Europe. As you are of course aware, at neither of these two institutions are solo calls ever permitted.

I have found the solo calls that have now for some years been the practice at the Metropolitan to be the most unsatisfactory and undignified. Arias and solo numbers give ample opportunity for the public to reward artists with individual applause. The practice of solo calls is widely used only in European provincial theaters, and there are, of course, good reasons why, as I said above, La Scala, Vienna and other leading opera houses will not permit solo calls at the end of acts or performances.

I feel sure that you will agree and collaborate with me by accepting the abolition of solo calls. We will make careful arrangements for group calls at the end of each act and performance and I am certain that the individual success of our distinguished artists will by no means suffer through that procedure while the general level of the House will be raised.

I want to exclude from this arrangement the opening night. This is a very special occasion in many ways and we will have solo calls for the opening night, but from then on

no solo calls will be permitted. Your cooperation is most earnestly requested.

Kind regards.

I was never engaged in "racing." I was not
upset if a singer sang elsewhere in this country
before the Met. So certainly it was no surprise
when Joan Sutherland—now Dame Joan—made
an instant success in her Met debut as Lucia. The
public went mad. Technically she was unique and
her high notes brought audiences to their feet.

Régine Crespin, a remarkable singer, showed
her artistry not only in French parts, but sang
equally well in the German and Italian repertory.

No one can admire Jon Vickers more than I
do, but I am aware that he has not the sweet voice
for the Duke in *Rigoletto* or Rodolfo in *Bohème*. His
Tristan and Otello, to mention two of his best
parts, are overwhelming. His Peter Grimes is exceptional. His intelligence and outstanding acting
ability make him stand head and shoulders above
most of his tenor colleagues.

Montserrat Caballé has one of the most beautiful voices of present-day sopranos. Her top legato
is almost unmatched. Her floating pianissimi en-
rapture the House. But dramatically she cannot
reach the vocal level.

I think that Fedora Barbieri and Fiorenza
Cossotto were two of the outstanding mezzos of my

time. They excited our audiences in a great variety of parts. Marilyn Horne is a mezzo any international opera house can be proud to present.

Irene Dalis and Nell Rankin both made their debuts as Eboli in *Don Carlo.* For years they were most useful to the Met.

Lisa Della Casa and Jarmila Novotna, in addition to being serious and excellent singers, were both beautiful to look at.

Risë Stevens deserves, in my view, a very special mention. Not only was she an exquisite artist, but even now, when she no longer sings, she helps the Met in many ways as Adviser on Young Artist Development.

Richard Tucker, America's leading tenor, was on a concert tour with his friend Robert Merrill when he suddenly and totally unexpectedly died. Needless to say, Tucker was an enormous loss to the Met. Not only was he a decent, friendly, helpful man—full of good humor—his was one of the great tenor voices. Irreplaceable.

And there was Eleanor Steber, who for many years was a reigning queen among our sopranos. She was an unequaled Mozart singer. Another unmatched Mozart singer is Nicolai Gedda, a great sylist. This does not mean that these two artists were not equally successful in a wide-ranging repertory.

There was Licia Albanese, for years the darling of the public. Anna Moffo is so lovely that she would have made a success even if she were not nearly as good a singer as she actually is. And Ettore Bastianini had one of the most beautiful baritone voices in my time. He died tragically young.

I cannot say too much about Jussi Bjoerling except that his was a great voice. However, he abused his health and altogether led an undisciplined life. It was always a struggle to make him come to any rehearsal.

Bjoerling died at the age of 49, his voice as beautiful as ever.

Another great tenor whom I was proud to have brought to the Met was Mario Del Monaco. When I heard him in San Francisco, I offered him one performance on his way back. In his eagerness to set foot on the Met stage, he accepted a somewhat lower fee. It was only later that he discovered that he never should have accepted such a fee and that others got more. He was very angry.

Of course I have not forgotten Zinka Milanov, one of the great voices of all time, who graced the stage of the Met until we moved into the new house.

We had many great singers at the Met. Some didn't stay long enough. Others stayed too long.

Many talented singers could not start at the Met. They had to launch their careers in various European houses. But Teresa Stratas came to the Met as an audition winner. She is an uncommon talent and personality with a lovely voice. She soon did major parts and went on to a world career.

Roberta Peters made her unscheduled debut on any opera stage, in the early days of my first season, as Zerlina in *Don Giovanni* replacing Nadine Conner a few hours before curtain time. She sang every season thereafter. I wrote to her shortly after her debut:

Dear Miss Peters:

I was very happy with the way you have discharged your sudden and heavy responsibility and only hope that you will now remain as sensible as you appear to be and not lose your sense of proportion. Your performance, however successful, does not make a career, so don't let photographers and reporters spoil you.

As far as your artistic work is concerned, we here shall try to further and help you and I am very hopeful for your development even though it may not always be as spectacular as the sudden chance of November 17.

A young American artist who made good with a big G, she too went on to a world career. Not all singers were the instant success Miss Peters was.

Yet I felt I should develop young artists—even more if they were American. To one promising young American singer I wrote in part:

In talking to Mr. Rudolf the other day about your place in the Metropolitan and your successful development as one of our leading singers, I was distressed to hear that you apparently were under the impression that I was not particularly pleased with your work.

Frankly, I cannot understand why you should have felt that and let me assure you that you were quite wrong. I thought that I had proved my respect for your efforts by giving you one excellent part after another.

It would be untrue if I said that I liked all of your work equally well, but on the whole I think you are doing a fine job and I am hopeful that your development will continue to progress. I shall certainly do all I can to help you, though it is inevitable that the repertory must fluctuate from season to season and that not every season can be as spectacular in activity as last season was.

I am particularly glad that you will do the role we discussed. I realize that this is not one of the spectacular parts but it is a very important part and the casting of such parts determines the artistic level of an opera house. It will do you credit to do such a part. You are sufficiently established as a leading artist to be able to afford it. After all, it is *how* a part is done that shows the ability of an artist, not *which* part is done.

On the whole, I would like you to feel that this management, including myself, is aware of your good work, is interested in your development and that you have nothing to worry about.

All singers have basic rules they have to learn. Certain singers take to it like ducks to water. And while there is excellent voice instruction in the United States, there is too little opportunity for practical experience. Consequently music schools must be more selective in accepting students.

When I met a young American singer some years ago, he stated he never would have thought he'd be singing at the Met. I wouldn't have either.

One of the unforgettable performances at the Met came from an actor, not a singer. It was Alfred Lunt who directed and appeared in *Così Fan Tutte*. For those who may be astonished to read about his "appearance," let me remind you that in the premiere of the new production in 1951, he appeared at the beginning of the opera in an exquisite costume and lit the lamps which adorned the front of the stage. The impression he made was what only a great actor could achieve.

Speaking of Alfred Lunt reminds me of the differences between singers and actors, apart from the obvious fact that one performer sings and the other speaks. Needless to say, no generalization is possible, but I think certain basic differences are established.

I would dare to state that, in general, actors have a higher level of intelligence, if for no other reason than that they have at one time or another read Shakespeare and other great playwrights. I venture to guess that there are many singers who have never heard of Shakespeare. While that does not necessarily imply a lack of intelligence, it does mean a lower level of interest.

Singers, on the whole, will know only the operas in which there are suitable parts for them. And indeed they may not know much more about the opera itself. They may know the plot, but many do not know their partner's part. Many singers are mainly concerned with learning melodies. Learning the music of long parts certainly requires an intellectual level, but I do maintain that learning Verdi arias is somewhat easier than learning a Shakespeare role.

Also, singers have to lead a more careful life. The vocal cords and their treatment is such an all-absorbing occupation or rather, let me say, such an all-absorbing worry that there simply is no time and no room for other considerations. Their careers, in a way, depend on two small vocal cords. Any cool breeze may upset them. Actors don't find it necessary not to talk all day prior to a performance.

But the singer's worry about the vocal cords naturally extends to movement if you want to call it acting. Of course many actors do not know what to do with their hands. Most singers, in my opinion, do not know what to do with anything.

Nothing can stop an actor saying what he has to say regardless of the movement that goes with the speech. But a singer, when he delivers an aria, has not only to watch the conductor to keep in time with the orchestra but also has to keep his movements under such control that they don't interfere with the delivery of a certain note, which may require all his attention.

In acting, there hardly ever occurs anything approaching what in opera is very frequent—ensembles. There the singer must not only worry about his own problems but he must watch his colleagues to be in tune and in line with them. Not to mention the conductor and the orchestra.

I think it is fair to say that, quite regardless of talent, singing opera demands more from a singer than acting does from an actor, intellect notwithstanding.

Both actor and singer share the difference in

the behavior of artists on stage and in private life. On stage they are nervously doing their job, while in private they think they can command the respect of everybody.

This too cannot be generalized. I do know quite a number of medium-quality artists who tremble before they are pushed on stage. As soon as they get off they behave as if they had performed a miracle.

SIX

WHEN ASKED IF the Met is the greatest opera house in the world, I answer that it once was but it cannot survive very much longer without federal subsidy. There are those who feel that "entertainment" that requires any subsidy other than what it can raise by selling sufficient tickets has no right to exist.

Fortunately, their number is small and getting smaller. The public has long realized that opera simply cannot exist without substantial subsidy. I cannot accept the premise of no subsidy. It has to come and I am sure, in due course, it will. Why?

No opera can exist without a large orchestra. I am not talking of some little provincial company which, incidentally, also requires subsidy. I am talking of large companies in large cities in the

United States and in Europe. The basic difference between the United States and Europe is that every company in Europe is fully subsidized by the State or the city—and, in some cases, both.

In addition to the orchestra, a company also requires a chorus. While the size varies, one may count on an orchestra of sixty or seventy members. The Met, Vienna, Berlin, etc., have nearly a hundred or more. And about the same applies to the chorus.

Without going into the details of salaries, it must be clear that the salaries of these groups represent high amounts. In addition to the basic weekly wage, there come many "extras" like overtime, afternoon performances and various other additions to the weekly basic wage.

Star singers are usually more highly paid than star actors, if for no other reason than that singers cannot perform more than twice, or three times at most, a week while actors usually give some eight performances a week. On rare occasions, certain singers demanded more than the highest fee being offered at the Met. If we could not meet their demands, they wouldn't sing. Singers go where the money is.

The budget of an opera performance is three or four times that of a play. Ticket prices can be more expensive at the opera, but even a sold-out house, as we so often had at the Met, cannot come near the expense.

Yet I don't know how subsidy would even-

tually work and I think it would be a little pre-
sumptuous to guess ahead of time.

A large part of the deficit is met by private
donations. In the last years, contributions by the
state via the Arts Council and the National Endow-
ment for the Arts have substantially increased. But
at the time of this writing a new threat of cuts
overshadows the arts.

I question whether it is desirable that these
organizations should take over the whole deficit. I
would think they will want a decisive influence on
the artistic policies. That is the danger.

Naturally, Management should do all they can
to keep costs down. One cost, among many that
cannot be avoided, is paying "cover singers." Even
small parts have to be covered, because without an
Angelotti, *Tosca* cannot go on.

If there is a performer involved in a pivotal
role and no alternate is available, Management—at
least mine—will have an alternate opera planned.
The artists for the alternate performances are
notified that they have to hold themselves available
and let management know where they can be
found in an emergency.

Of course, in a repertory house like the Met,
the problem is aggravated by the subscription
series. If the performance has to be changed and it
turns out that the alternate opera was played on
the same series only two or three weeks ago, still
another opera has to be found.

A few seasons back, after I left the Met,

Leontyne Price was forced to cancel a performance of *Ariadne auf Naxos*. My thoughts turned to my various colleagues at the Met and what they went through. There are *some* advantages to not being at the Met anymore.

The first thought was: who can replace Price? Singers of her quality generally are not available, and, in fact, there are not too many around. In addition, *Ariadne* is just not a regular repertoire opera. One could, at least in my time, find a Mimi or a Tosca without too much difficulty, but there are not too many Ariadnes available. So they may have to turn to changing the performance and, in this case, they did, to the new production of *Don Carlo*.

This production, however, had more than new scenery and costumes. It had an added act, which Verdi himself had taken out after the Paris production. Now, that is the Management's right, but it adds about forty minutes' playing time. *Don Carlo,* even without this act, is a long opera. This new production played from 7:15 to nearly midnight.

Fine. But now back to the *Ariadne* cancellation. *Ariadne* happens to be a very short opera starting at the usual 8:00 curtain. Obviously they could not change the time because many patrons do not read the evening paper or listen to the radio and were perfectly entitled to see an opera starting at 8:00. And there was the problem.

They had to start *Don Carlo* at 8:00, which resulted in enormous overtime. There are fifteen unions involved. There is a full orchestra, a large chorus, the stagehands, electricians, wardrobe—not to forget the front-of-House staff. It must have been a staggering amount of overtime.

In addition, *Don Carlo* had just been performed the night before. Only one singer repeated her performance. There were also three unscheduled Met debuts, all in leading roles.

The rule at the Metropolitan is that change of cast does not entitle the ticketholder to a refund, but a change of opera does. I was sorry to hear that crowds requested refunds. So you can see the consequences a cancellation can cause.

It was an unhappy night for the Met.

🖵🖵

Among the many things that have changed over the past years in opera management is the planning of a season.

When I joined the Met, one could plan a full season eight or ten months ahead. Today, one has to plan three or four years ahead.

What happened? What is the reason?

It started in my time at the Met. If I wanted a particular singer and discovered that he or she was engaged elsewhere, I would approach the next singer I wanted a year earlier. And so the mad circus started.

Indeed, in many cases, one cannot be sure that the voice will be the same three or four years later. If one is dealing with singers in their twenties or thirties, there is a good chance that the voice will still be good. However, if one deals with a singer in his or her forties or older, there is no certainty that the three or four years may not make a serious difference.

It is a risk one has to take these days. That risk may by diminished if the singer concerned is famous and beloved by the public, who are more likely to overlook, or even ignore, the deterioration.

The availability of singers naturally plays a role in assembling a season's repertory—one of the most important and difficult tasks of any manager. There are a million considerations. How do you start? I used to start setting up a "dream repertory," then eliminating one work after another, which for some reason could not be done.

One of the first considerations has to be a look at the repertory of the last two or three seasons. What important works have been done too little or too much or not at all? How was the balance between Italian, French or German operas? How many operas of the most prominent composers— Verdi, Puccini, Mozart, Wagner, etc.—have been seen? And then the eternal problem of whether a contemporary opera should be included came up.

This process gives a first broad outline of which works should or should not be considered.

Almost at the same time, the casts come under consideration. There was not much point in planning *Tristan und Isolde* unless you were sure of having superb singers for those parts available— and available at the time you needed them.

The manager must consider who of the established stars or promising singers will be around? Who should he try to engage? Who deserves some special "plum"—opening night, new productions, radio broadcasts—and now television? These of course are the most important and most obvious "plums."

Every General Manager faces an interesting problem—artistic quality versus the box office. There are, of course, some artists and operas which don't present the problem.

The box office has to be studied. What operas seem to have more or less exhausted their appeal? What operas have not been done in some time and should be done again? Most important, which works deserve or need a new production, and what designers, directors and conductors are available? This is where a General Manager has to let his imagination run wild.

Availability makes plans possible or not. If you have at last settled for one opera, is the conductor you choose available at the same time as the director? Not to mention the singers.

The ideal arrangement would be to get everyone you want and get the contracts out. But it just doesn't work that way. One has to compromise. And just when some sort of vague repertory seems to emerge, the problem of subscriptions again raises its ugly head.

Obviously no subscription series can have the same opera twice. Also, the subscription has to be made attractive by giving the audience a fair share of Italian and other popular operas. You have to avoid, for instance, even if it fits in with other plans, giving them three Wagner operas in a row. And then, when it all eventually takes shape, the tenor announces that he cannot make himself available for the time you count on him.

The planning of a new production repeats the problems of planning a repertory on a somewhat smaller scale. Again one starts with the ideal hopes. Then one has to cope with the inevitable disappointments. This artist is already booked. This designer has no wish to work with that director. This conductor doesn't want this particular singer. And conductors would generally fight it out in a new production. If he wasn't a Karajan, or someone of his caliber, chances were he was just told to go to hell.

There were always those who wondered why I did not produce such-and-such and engage so-and-so. When asked why I cast so-and-so as such-and-such, my usual answer was "in despair." As I have said, I did let my imagination run wild, but there were many times when I simply could not achieve what I wished, for whatever reason.

There were quite a few operas that I wished to produce and never did and many artists whom I invited to the Met who, for one reason or another, never came. There were also artists at the Met for whom I had certain roles in mind but who, for whatever reason, never sang.

For one example, when I mounted the new production of *Ariadne auf Naxos,* it was meant for Birgit Nilsson. Unfortunately, she never sang the role, but luckily we also had Leonie Rysanek and Lisa Della Casa who shared the part. And it was well known that the new production of *Nabucco* was meant for Leonard Warren, who died on stage the year before. Jussi Bjoerling was asked to sing Radames in *Aïda* in a season he eventually canceled.

Among the artists I tried to engage but didn't succeed was Victor de Sabata to conduct *Turandot* when Mitropoulos died. Dietrich Fischer-Dieskau was asked to sing Wolfram in *Tannhäuser.* Sir Frederick Ashton was my first choice for *Martha* and Sir John Gielgud for *Don Pasquale.* I also asked Jerome Robbins for the same opera. There were many more who were approached through my twenty-two years.

I even at one time considered producing *The Merry Widow,* and I asked Cecil Beaton to design it.

It is not an easy job.

And, of course, the operas that needed or deserved new productions were immediately linked up to the budget. How much was donated specifically for new productions? Indeed, on occasion, a donor would give money for a specific production. So you either did the opera or lost the money—unless the donor could be persuaded to change his mind and leave the money for another work.

Negotiations got really tough and complicated when one dealt with a new production. At the Met, on average, we rehearsed three weeks. Then, hoping for a success and also depending on the type of work, we might wish to schedule eight performances within eight or ten weeks. In short, we needed the leading artists and the conductor for about thirteen weeks.

In thirteen weeks any leading singer would expect an average of twenty-six guaranteed performances. So we are short. In some cases, the privilege of singing in a new production at the Met would solve the situation. There was always the possibility of singing a role in another production, which would make up the guarantee.

The balance of the repertory very much depends on the availability of singers. The Met, for instance, does not have such staples as *Aïda* or *Carmen* in the repertory at the time of this writing. I don't agree that such popular operas or the like can't be cast satisfactorily. I think there's always a cast for these operas. It just has to be searched for and found.

An important consideration is that—somewhat contrary to the past—the public changes. In old times, subscribers had their seats for ten or more years. Newcomers just had to wait their turn.

That is not quite the same anymore. There is an influx of a new public. They should be able to see and hear the standard works. *Billy Budd* is a great opera, but it will not really draw a new public. It is a fact, whether we like it or not, that the vast majority of the public prefers the old and well-known operas and stays away from the new and contemporary. An even averagely cast *Bohème* or *Aïda* will outsell a better cast modern work.

In addition, one has to consider that the great stars are reluctant to let themselves be cast in contemporary works, which require hard study and long rehearsals with the prospect of few performances. If a tenor studies *Bohème* or *Aïda*, he knows he will sing that opera many times all over the world for many years to come. A singer who studies *Mourning Becomes Electra*, for example, has little chance of utilizing his labor sufficiently to make it worthwhile.

An unexpected and fortunately rare problem arose when a music publisher of a modern opera once tried to influence casting. I was annoyed when the publisher suggested that I should ex-change one of the leading singers for another one.

When I replied that I saw no reason for that change, but—if he liked—could drop the opera and do a Verdi work instead, he was suddenly very pleased with the casting.

Now, even with that knowledge, the management has a cultural obligation to show some lesser known operas and, in particular, to show contemporary works to further young composers. I say this, although looking back over my twenty-two years at the Met, I certainly cannot claim to be proud of my contribution to modern opera. The only contemporary operas which I felt were worth the trouble and the money were Alban Berg's *Wozzeck,* a masterpiece of our time, Benjamin Britten's *Peter Grimes,* a very close second, and Richard Strauss's *Arabella.*

It is hard to reconcile these two positions. Subscriptions of, say, eight performances, will do well if one contemporary opera is hidden among *Faust, Traviata, Tosca* or whatever. If there are three contemporary works with five "standard" works, I fear that subscription will not do too well.

There is just no clear answer, and the Manager has to take risks and decide whether he prefers good press and cultural success or a good box office. Naturally, that links up with the economic situation of his theater.

If he has sponsors who substantially contribute to the production of modern operas he may be able to take risks that a Manager with an old-fashioned and money-minded Board cannot afford.

SEVEN

NEEDLESS TO SAY, maintaining good relations with the press is a very important part of management. I cannot say I was very successful in that field. For some reason or other, I viewed the press as an enemy out to hurt me, if not necessarily the opera. I was always in trouble with the press. Nobody loved us but the public.

I am a foreigner who suddenly out of the blue was catapulted into the most important musical position in the United States. I was considered "cool" and "aloof." In meeting the press, I was particularly anxious not to appear as if I wanted something or was trying to "win them over." All of this was wrong and naturally did not improve my personal relationship with the various ladies and gentlemen of the press.

I confess I did not have great respect for them. I feel very strongly that hardly any music critics become critics by choice. It is hardly a profession a young man would choose unless there was some negative reason in the background. If somebody wanted to be a pianist, fiddler or a conductor and discovered that his talent was not sufficient for a professional career but that he had a talent for writing, music criticism would be a way out.

I can speak for myself. When I discovered my voice was not good enough for a professional career, I turned to management. But the unsuccessful pianist or fiddler who turns to criticism finds himself obliged to cover not only pianists and fiddlers, but also singers and opera performances for which he or she never had any preparation and really has not basic knowledge. Also, there may be some subconscious grudge against the more successful artists.

Surely anybody in the House has the right to his or her personal opinion about a singer, conductor or a performance. But the critic not only has his opinion, he voices it in print and we all know the power of the printed word.

As it happened, the critics had very little or no influence on *our* public. If they disliked a performance the press could write until they were blue in the face all sorts of negative opinions, but the public came despite them.

I remember the opposite situation, when we had some performances the press praised. The public stayed away in droves. The Metropolitan Opera subscribers were the same for generations. They knew what they liked and it was damned hard to change them.

In many cases I felt the press just had to criticize. That was their profession for which they were paid. And criticize they did.

I was particularly annoyed at one critic and said so to his managing editor at a major New York newspaper:

Dear Sir:

I am greatly embarrassed to have to write this letter but I would appreciate your view on a difficult problem.

The Metropolitan Opera's Management is under the impression that it still has the right to determine whom it wishes to be present at its dress rehearsals. In the case of a dress rehearsal for any new work or any work that has not been performed for a great many years, it is the practice to invite the press so that the critics may have a chance, if they so desire, to acquaint themselves with the work before they see it in the first performance which, incidentally, in most cases they cannot attend right to the end as they have to meet their deadlines.

In the case of the recent dress rehearsal of

The Barber of Seville we did not consider it necessary to invite the press because it cannot by any stretch of imagination be said that it would be necessary for critics to acquaint themselves with this work. For various reasons, therefore, we decided that the dress rehearsal should not be open to the press and no press invitations were sent out. On the contrary, when one or two of our friends on the press inquired, they were told that no press invitations had been sent out for this rehearsal and naturally these gentlemen respected our arrangements and did not appear.

Your critic did not make any previous inquiry but, on the other hand, appeared for the rehearsal with, if I am correctly informed, a party of three guests. When he was told by the person present in the Press Department that no press passes were being given out for the rehearsal, he just said that he did not need any tickets and entered the house with his guests. Naturally, I did not wish to aggravate the situation, which was embarrassing and unpleasant, by asking him to leave and he was, therefore, permitted to remain.

As you may have seen, in his review about the first performance he specifically referred to his presence at the dress rehearsal coupled with a derogatory remark about that rehearsal. Apart from the fact that critics, according to their code of etiquette, are expected not to report on rehearsals even when they are welcome to attend such rehearsals, it seems to me a gross violation of that code that a critic should refer to a rehearsal when it should have been quite clear to him that his presence was most unwelcome.

May I look to you for help in avoiding similar situations in the future?

Over the years the situation somewhat mellowed.

When I met Mr. Schonberg, who for many years was the leading critic for *The New York Times,* in the corridor, we actually had a friendly little talk. I recently had a pleasant luncheon with Mr. Kolodin who, in addition to being a distinguished critic, is the author of *The Metropolitan Opera.* Mr. Henahan who has succeeded Mr. Schonberg at the *Times* was reasonably friendly in his writings, but we hardly met.

Harriett Johnson and Speight Jenkins of the *New York Post* were usually friendly to me. Certainly Louis Biancolli, Irving Kolodin, Winthrop Sargeant and Miles Kastendieck were also helpful. That about covers the important press of New York.

Now I believe that they were all basically friendly and it was up to me to establish a reasonable relationship. Not doing so was one of my mistakes.

Needless to say there is no Manager who has not made mistakes. The measure of his success or failure depends on the magnitude and, in some cases, the timing of his mistakes.

There are innumerable areas within which mistakes can be made. The most visible and audible is, of course, in the realm of engaging soloists. If a tenor or soprano or indeed any other singer makes a bad impression in performance, that is the first thing the audience will notice. In due course they will notice, indirectly, mistakes in other departments. A bad design may be a matter of taste. That also applies to the director. Very much more noticeable is the conductor. A bad stage manager can louse up a performance without the public's noticing too much about it.

At one performance of *Don Carlo* there was a strange mistake in the first act. In the courtyard scene, Posa has managed that all the ladies-in-waiting disappear for a moment, giving Don Carlo a chance to talk to the Queen alone. At that moment the King enters. But just a second before the King was to appear, the stage manager, by mistake, sent all the ladies back to the stage from all sides. This made nonsense of the King's remark: "Why is the Queen alone and not even one lady with her?"

This is an important moment because it fur-

With Thomas Schippers on his debut night. I deeply regret the tragic and much too early end of his rising career. (*credit: Sedge LeBlang*)

Left, Jarmila Novotna as Octavian in *Der Rosenkavalier*. (*credit: Metropolitan Opera Archives*)

Right, Richard Tucker as Rodolfo in Verdi's *Luisa Miller*. (*credit: Louis Melançon*)

Left, Jon Vickers in the title role of Verdi's *Otello*. (*credit: Metropolitan Opera Archives*)

Right, Teresa Stratas as Cherubino in *Nozze di Figaro*. (*credit: Louis Melançon*)

With Maria Callas. (*credit: Louis Melançon*)

In my office with Sol Hurok. (*credit: Louis Melançon*)

Anthony Bliss, the current General Manager of the Met, with three ex-Managers: Kurt Herbert Adler of San Francisco, the late Carol Fox of Chicago and myself. (*credit: Metropolitan Opera Archives*)

Right, Presenting Osie Hawkins with a silver clock on his twenty-fifth anniversary with the Met. (*credit: Louis Melançon*); *Below*, Presenting roses to Zinka Milanov at her farewell performance as Maddalena in *Andrea Chénier*. Richard Tucker holds her silver tray. (*credit: Metropolitan Opera Archives*)

A kiss from Nina on the opening night of the new Met. (*credit: Metropolitan Opera Archives*)

With my friend Marc Chagall in front of one of his two murals in the new Met, prior to the official opening. (*credit: Metropolitan Opera Archives*)

thers the King's suspicion, and it is up to the stage manager to time the reentrance of the ladies in such a way that the King's remark makes sense.

Mistakes can also be made by designers and directors as for instance at a performance of *Lohengrin* that I attended. Lohengrin appears in the first act, and the first sign of his "God-sent" mission is that he recognizes Elsa, whom he has never seen, among the ladies. Now, if all the ladies are in various costumes and only one in white stands out, it seems very easy for him to recognize her. There should be six or eight ladies in white standing around. Then it is a "miracle" that he picks out the right one.

I was forever conscious of the stage manager's role as the following memos demonstrate:

To the Stage Manager:

We did talk yesterday about getting chorus, ballet, etc., down in time so that rehearsals can start punctually and not, as they have done lately, three or four or five minutes late.

I wonder what happened with the intermissions yesterday? I had originally suggested that they should be twenty-three minutes each but then yesterday morning we agreed that they should be twenty minutes each and that the performance should start at 8:05. It started at 8:08—why? And the first intermission was 26½ minutes, the second intermission 27½ minutes. Surely the scene change could not have been the cause for running into overtime so badly.

What is all this sudden lapse of discipline? Would you please discuss it with your colleagues and let me know whether there are any reasons and, if so, what can be done at once to improve the situation?

To the Stage Manager:

I would be grateful please if, before undertaking any basic changes on the revival productions requested by stage directors, this would first be checked with me. I am referring particularly to the new benches that have been asked for in the second act of *Tannhäuser*. Had I known of this in advance I would most likely have persuaded the gentleman in charge to refrain from putting them in. I don't think they improve the picture—on the contrary— and I don't think they serve any useful purpose. They have, however, cost time, labor and money.

I am not referring, of course, to tiny little things here and there about which I do not want to be bothered. But if it comes to changing something or introducing something rather basically in a production that has existed for quite some time, then I want to be notified before it is done.

To the Stage Manager:

During the second act of today's performance of *Rigoletto,* during the "Caro nome" aria, I had to telephone from my box to the stage and ask for quiet backstage because I could hear talking up to my box from the 40th Street Side where the male chorus were assembling for their entrance.

The lack of backstage discipline has now reached dimensions which cannot be allowed to continue unchecked. We are deteriorating to an amateur theater. Will you please immediately after the New Year set up a meeting with the gentlemen in charge and the chorus delegates. Please see to it that I am advised because I want to attend.

To the Stage Manager:

As you know, for the orchestra every minute or two going into the next quarter of an hour is counted, by contract, as a full quarter of an hour. Consequently even only one or two minutes can amount to large overtime payments. Therefore, I wish you would turn your attention now to punctual start of rehearsals.

This was very good last season and even at the beginning of this season, but now we are back to rehearsals, including orchestra rehearsals, starting three, four, five or more minutes late. So far I have not obtained any satisfactory explanation for the delay. I am either told that bells in the chorus dressing room did not function or that the elevator was busy or that the ballet ladies "refuse to come down." I, in turn, refuse to believe the latter; as far as the bells are concerned, they ought to be checked, and as far as the elevators are concerned, perhaps arrangements could be made for the elevators to hold themselves available five to eight minutes prior to commencement of a rehearsal. And, apart from that, I cannot consider it a particular hardship for chorus or ballet to walk *down* if the elevator happens to be busy.

Be that as it may, I would be grateful if everyone concerned would please turn their attention to getting rehearsals again to start sharp on time. Thank you.

To the Stage Manager:

The incredible occurrence of last night when Mr. Anthony's absence was discovered approximately an hour too late leads me to suspect that there is either no or faulty organization of backstage arrangements. I would like you please to let me know who is responsible for checking that all artists arrive in accordance with the house rules. If there is more than one person responsible for this checking, how is the division made and do the persons concerned know for what group they are responsible and is there no danger that one may believe that another is responsible for something which in fact he himself is supposed to do?

I realize that mistakes can happen—I am making them myself—but there are certain mistakes that ought not to happen.

The other day I remember you yourself telling me that an intermission had to be extended because one of the participating artists (I forget who it was) was not ready. What is the organization to keep you informed in very good time about the progress in dressing rooms, that is to say, how far artists have advanced in their changes, in their makeup, etc? We are wasting a good deal of time, particularly in rehearsals and perhaps also in performances, in extending intermissions beyond the necessary duration by not being firm enough in chasing artists for changes, dressing, etc. It is not your responsibility to run around to dressing rooms to inquire how far an artist has got, but it is your responsibility to organize things in such a way that you are continuously informed by your subordinates so that you can take personal charge whenever that seems necessary.

I shall be grateful if you will please look into your complete backstage organization and either initiate or overhaul arrangements so that the possibility of an incident like last night's or similar incidents is reduced to an absolute minimum.

The two main foundations on which opera is built are artistic and economic. They are indissolubly linked. Finance and art cannot easily be separated. Every artistic decision is reflected in the budget and every financial decision has some influence on the artistic side of the operation. When an artistic manager is convinced that a particular singer has the right qualifications for a particular production and the business manager is convinced that the terms of that singer are not acceptable—who decides? Obviously the General Manager.

Artists are sensitive and easily offended. Particularly among themselves, they are apt to make a mountain of a molehill. In such cases, it is the Manager's job to try to reestablish peace, which is essential to smooth collaboration among all parties.

You don't need wit to run an opera house. You need style.

How does a General Manager establish any kind of relationship with his Company? I suppose as many managers as there are, that many relationships exist.

As I said before, I was rather cool but that didn't mean I was disinterested. Inevitably personal contacts arise—much as I tried to avoid them. You cannot help being drawn to one person more than to another. I did successfully avoid "friendships." Artists are, by nature, jealous. As soon as they see the Manager and an artist with more than a superficial relationship, rumors spread immediately. The whole company can get into turmoil.

If the artist concerned gets one or more leading parts—however pure the motives— nothing will persuade the company that it is not a "liaison" that is behind it all. The whole spirit of the company can be destroyed.

I remember that a distinguished European artist, prior to her arrival at the Met, inquired about the "intrigues" in the house. Frankly I really didn't know what she meant. But, needless to say, in a big opera company, just as in any big company, there are certain intrigues going on. As far as I'm concerned, I am unaware that I ever knowingly got involved with intrigue or made decisions on the basis of intrigue. Feuds were not part of my daily routine. Nor was fund raising.

While, on the whole, I feel I did not do too badly over twenty-two years at the Met, how many mistakes did I make? It might be best to try to subdivide the mistakes of casting, conducting, repertory, designers and directors.

I produced in my tenure almost eighty new productions in addition to the so-called "revised" productions and the many revivals. Quickly thinking *The Rake's Progress* was perhaps the most serious mistake. We all know that Stravinsky was one of the greatest composers of our time. Yet the work misfired.

One proof may be that it very quickly disappeared not only from the repertory of the Met but from almost all opera houses anywhere, though there is an occasional revival or two.

In spite of the quality of Fritz Reiner who conducted and George Balanchine who directed, the opera was pretty disastrous. We had seven performances in two seasons at about half a house for most. It never appeared again at the Met.

Flotow's *Martha* was certainly a mistake. It is an

undistinguished opera which I did only for Victoria De Los Angeles. But her beautiful singing was not enough even with Richard Tucker as her tenor. Carl Ebert was just wasted on this fluffy little piece. The conductor, Nino Verchi, could not do much to rescue the work.

After the enormous success of *Fledermaus,* I tried *The Gypsy Baron.* But not even Johann Strauss is infallible. Perhaps it also was not too good a performance. At any rate, it failed.

According to the press there was one mistake with which I don't agree. Jean-Louis Barrault's *Carmen* was torn to pieces for reasons I never understood. Nobody will consider the opera a mistake. I didn't consider the production one either. The name Barrault will long be remembered when the names of some of his critics will long be forgotten.

I wonder what the critics would have written had I been able to get my first choice to direct this opera—Charlie Chaplin.

I obviously would not like to mention singers and conductors who proved flops. But of course there were some. Who am I not to have made mistakes in twenty-two years?

I was fiercely against the New York City

Opera's becoming a constituent of Lincoln Center and said so to the Board as early as 1960. The Board disagreed with me and I had no choice but to accept the decision.

Rereading my memo to the Board after twenty-one years, I admit that my assumptions were wrong. Lincoln Center has in no way suffered by the inclusion of the New York City Opera and the New York City Ballet. Indeed these two organizations have contributed to the general standard of Lincoln Center.

At times, too much pressure brought out a certain stubbornness in me that delayed decision. I am not necessarily proud of this but it is a truthful statement. One such delay was not hiring Birgit Nilsson earlier than I did. She wouldn't have been so expensive. Once, when asked if Miss Nilsson was difficult, I answered: "Not at all. You put enough money in and glorious sound comes out."

I read somewhere that Beverly Sills was quoted as saying: "At least he admits his mistakes."

And I do.

In the beginning of my Met days, I made a point of being in the House at every performance. In later years the singers *thought* I was there. I did attend rehearsals most of the time. So by opening night of each production there were very little surprises.

Some conductors thought they could do everything. It was interesting to watch the musicians. If the conductor was Karajan, they would sit on the edges of their chairs. For some "house" conductors, they would slump. Most good conductors prefer the concert business, where they earn in only three days a higher fee than they get for the four weeks necessary to prepare an opera. And they don't have to share the glamor with the soprano.

And some directors also thought they could do everything. The director's work is in some ways the most difficult because he works exclusively from his own inspiration. While the conductor and the singers have a musical score, the director has a blank space he must populate with his cast, who for the most part, don't understand what he wants.

We had three types of directors working at the Met. And we were lucky to have some very distinguished ones in all three categories. For the best directors are, in their way, just as important as singers, if not more so.

For the "guest" category, I have no hesitation in turning straight to Franco Zeffirelli. He is not only a director full of spirited imagination but also a brilliant designer. His *Falstaff* and *Otello* are unforgettable creations. He also directed a brilliant *Cav* and *Pag*. He works with singers with so much charm and, at the same time, firmness that he gets them to do exactly what he wants. I think Zeffirelli stands at the top of the international list of designers and directors, and I am proud I brought him to the Met.

For our "house team" we had Nat Merrill and

Bob O'Hearn who, at least in my time, almost always worked together. They produced nothing but successes. Perhaps they did not quite reach the unique originality that Zeffirelli always displayed, but they always worked on a high level of taste and were real professionals. It also didn't hurt to have two young Americans display their art.

Herbert Graf was at the Met when I came and left many years later. If he was not the imaginative and spirited director others were, Graf was a total professional and everything he did had distinction.

Garson Kanin was my second "Broadway" director, Margaret Webster having been the first with *Don Carlo* on my opening night.

He directed *Fledermaus* and kept it within the Viennese tradition yet invented an amusing touch of Broadway. Each time we revived this production—and it was one of the most revived productions—I tried to give it a fresh look. When we moved into the new house, I was delighted that Kitty Carlisle accepted my invitation to sing Orlofsky, taking time off from her important duties with the New York State Council on the Arts.

But we also needed directors for the upkeep of our earlier productions. The result of these upkeeps were really dependent on the "book" kept by the original director.

There were four permanently engaged assistant stage directors through the years: Bodo Igesz, Nikolaus Lehnhoff, Fabrizio Melano and Patrick

Tavernia. Whenever a "guest" director worked on a new production one of the assistants was assigned to him. It was his duty to supervise the "regiebook" kept by the stage manager. In that book all the moves and positions of the individual artists were recorded.

Once the first performance was over, the "guest" director usually left. Then it was up to the assistant to supervise the subsequent performances and in particular to restage the work in a later season as near as possible to the original performance. It was also their function to rehearse the understudies so that they were ready at any time to step in.

While no one can deny the beauty of the old Met's auditorium, it was not a practical opera house if one considers the technical equipment needed to produce an effective performance. So, while we were able to mount the beautiful *Falstaff* there thanks to Zeffirelli's skill, there was no way we could have produced *Die Frau ohne Schatten* in the old House.

Backstage in an opera house or, indeed, in any theater is a world of its own.

At the new Met there is the centerstage. Then there are two stages, left and right of the center, and a fourth stage behind—all of equal size. The *Die Frau ohne Schatten* production utilized all four stages, plus in one scene the stage floor rose to the fly area as yet another stage came up from beneath.

It was a spectacular production and an enormous success. I was delighted.

Of course, the stage equipment could also be used in much more simple productions. For instance, in *La Bohème,* the first act set is the same as the fourth. In the old House, the first-act set had to be dismantled, stored and then rebuilt. Now one can just push this set to one side or to the back. When it comes again, it is simply rolled on.

Who does all that? The head of the backstage area is the stage manager, who in the end is responsible for every scene—not only for the sets and the props, but also of course for the singers, who must be where they ought to be at the right moment.

In my time, Osie Hawkins was the world's most conscientious stage manager, who would rather die than leave his desk during a performance. He knew his operas backward and one could rely on his signals' coming to the right quarter at the right time with complete assurance.

None of the productions could be possible without the stagehands. If I remember correctly, there were nearly eighty at the Met. In addition to setting and striking acts, they are responsible for packing and unpacking the productions to and from the warehouses.

The wardrobe staff is responsible for seeing to it that all singers find the right costumes in their dressing rooms and indeed, with complicated costumes, for helping them get dressed in time. The wig staff has the same duties as far as hairdress is concerned.

It would be somewhat embarrassing if pens, letters, glasses, handbags, handkerchiefs, guns and the like—so important in the plots of operas—were missing on stage. The prop department is responsible for preventing that.

A very important position is that of the head electrician, who is responsible for all the lighting. He works closely with the designer and director, who tell him what mood they want for every scene and the way they want the singers lit. A good chief electrician can do a great deal to enhance the beauty of a production.

When Marc Chagall designed our *Die Zauberflöte*, he attended every rehearsal and in fact painted a good deal of the production himself. Naturally, for him the electrician is particularly important.

Chagall approved of our lighting and our switchboard. He was very satisfied that we could create the proper colors and moods. So was I.

In fact, I tried to get Chagall in the old House. In 1955 I wrote:

My dear Marc:

I have a crazy idea! Next season we are planning to present a 20- or 25-minute little ballet to charming music by Rossini in a modern adaptation by Benjamin Britten. It is called *Soirées Musicales* and this is the title we will give the ballet, which will have no story but consist merely of pas de deux, pas de trois and this sort of thing. Would you consider designing for me a backdrop? This is all we need. There will be no scenery, just the flat stage and a wonderful backdrop with fitting legs to mask. The measurements are approximately 60 × 40.

Naturally I cannot afford to pay you what you would normally ask. On the other hand, I think this may take you not much more than an afternoon's work. I just want a few lovely Chagall colors—that's all. We would need the sketch early in September. Do let me know what you think of it and what you would want for it.

Hoping to see you soon and very much hoping for your backdrop. It would be a matter of great pride to me to be able to have a Chagall design in one of my seasons.

All best.

Though Chagall declined *Soirées Musicales,* years later I was fortunate to obtain his services.

While I was working in a bookstore in my early years in Vienna, a thin volume on Marc Chagall appeared. I saw for the first time these flying cows and blue horses with the half-moon somewhere at the bottom of the picture and a little cockerel in an upper corner. It was then that I fell in love with that childlike magic world of Marc Chagall; it never occurred to me that I might meet the painter.

Frankly, I never thought of the man behind all these strange figures—but as time went by I—all of us—saw and heard more and more about Marc Chagall.

When Nina and I moved to Berlin, we met a charming young Russian woman: Vava Brodzky. Vava and Nina became great friends and after a while we all met again in London. Years went and the war came. We all went through hard times. Vava too did not have it easy, but we always kept in close touch and, in spite of all the terror and worries, we laughed a lot together.

Then the war came to an end. I started the Edinburgh Festival and eventually in 1949 went to America. Naturally contact with Vava slipped a little, but we kept in touch and met in Paris from time to time. For a while we did not hear from her, and then came the sensational news: Vava was to be married to Marc Chagall. And soon we met him and have been great friends ever since.

Chagall is the kind of man one either knows well or not at all. After the first ten minutes one feels as if one had known each other all one's life and even after a year's absence one feels as if one had met only yesterday.

We met almost every year, in Paris, in Switzerland, in their house in Vence or in New York. Naturally we talked often about music, about ballet and opera; I knew he loved Mozart perhaps more than any other music.

I started thinking about the repertory for the first season in our new house at least three years ahead of time; I had some years before produced a *Magic Flute* in the old house, but I had not been happy with that production, even though Bruno Walter conducted it at the time. I was determined to do this—one of my favorite operas—again and it occurred to me that Chagall's magic world might be the right foil for Mozart's magic. I had engaged Günther Rennert, the eminent German stage director, for the production, and he enthusiastically endorsed my suggestion, so I approached Chagall and he showed great interest but also great concern.

He knew this was a great challenge—he had never done sets and costumes for an opera—but also a great responsibility. I told him that I thought he would enjoy working with Rennert, that we had an excellent painter—a Russian (Volodia Odinokov) as the head of our paint shop, and that we would give him all the help and support he might require. Then I asked Rennert to visit him in Vence, and as I had hoped and expected—I also sent him a recording of *The Magic Flute*—he soon was deeply involved and drew and painted sketches from morning to night.

We soon reached agreement; he had several more meetings with Rennert, then he came to New York, met the painters, the tailors and saw the stage—and the result is now history.

At the same time, the new House was being built and there were two large areas on the Grand Tier foyer that required artistic treatment. Wallace Harrison, our distinguished architect, gave it a great deal of thought, together with our Art Committee, and innumerable ideas were advanced and discarded.

At the same time I suggested the possibility of two large Chagall murals, and eventually everyone concerned liked the idea. Chagall was again invited to come over. He inspected the site, he met the Art Committee, and finally he was commissioned to paint these murals—a commission made possible by the generous contribution of funds by Mr. Newlin on behalf of the Doherty Foundation, just as Mrs. John D. Rockefeller, Jr., had made it possible for us to produce *The Magic Flute.*

So here we are with a *Magic Flute,* designed by Marc Chagall, the only Opera House in the world that can boast a Marc Chagall production and two huge Chagall murals—and I for one am proud of it.

We had many other distinguished designers. Rolf Gérard did the greatest number of productions for me. Caspar Neher made a great impression with some of his designs.

But when one of the Met's most important designers was unhappy with his advance publicity for one of our new productions, I wrote in part:

It is quite true that for one of the other productions the Press Department has attempted more advance publicity. Unfortunately, I was too late informed about these plans because had I known of them I would have stopped them. Unfortunately, some of this, in my view, quite stupid advance publicity appeared and did all the harm that I expected it would.

Why do you not rely on the quality of your work to wait for publicity and favorable comment? I am dead against all this advance bally-hoo even though it may be the custom in America. If I have learned one thing here it is that neither the press nor the public wants to be told in advance "how wonderful" a coming production or a coming singer is. You are aware of the singer who recently made a debut, who was another glaring example of the inadvisability of this type of advance publicity. Here was an artist of outstanding merit and quality who was badly built up by telling everybody in advance how good he was and as a result he was a complete flop here—the one and only place in the world where he was built up in advance and where he proved a failure.

You are by no means ignored. On the contrary, you are looked upon by myself and everyone in this House as a most important contributor to whatever success my Management has been able to achieve. As far as I am concerned, as you rightly say, I have proved that, by continually offering you new assignments even though you have by no means been over-cooperative in that respect. You have always picked exclusively what you wanted to do and have not once chosen to be helpful to me in accepting an assignment which I wanted you to do even though you were not particularly keen on it. I am not blaming you for that, but you cannot blame me for noticing it.

However, this has nothing to do with the point at issue. The same sort of releases were issued as for any other production. The designer in question had a personal press agent here who, as I said, much to my regret and with by no means advantageous results, managed to get a certain amount of special publicity. If you had such a press agent I could not prevent you, though I would try my best, from having similar advance publicity. I am confident that your work will get all the credit it deserves.

It is surprising that no more goes wrong in opera. It is something bordering on the miraculous that everybody in a production really feels involved, however minute his or her job may be. And what is the main thing, they do their jobs well and with pleasure. Enthusiasm simmers down right from the General Manager to the boy who supervises the spear carriers.

But with all the miracles in back of the House, there are those who work in the front with responsibility. There is the box-office staff who, needless to say, take in a great portion of the income over the window. There are the ticket-takers who help the patrons, the ushers who show you to your seat. Then there are the security staff, the concessions, such as the restaurant and the bars, and the cleaners who put the House in order after every performance.

So you see it is quite a big operation. It is amazing to think of the sheer quantity of people employed in an opera house.

EIGHT

TODAY ARTISTS ARE different, as is management. In my early days, singers still had moral and artistic integrity, and agents were businessmen interested only in making an engagement for an artist to any theater and collecting their commissions. This gradually changed.

I think the role of the manager found its high point in Ronald Wilford—no doubt the most important, most able and most interesting man in New York's musical life. He is one of those rare men in music who does not want fame. On the contrary, he avoids it. Yet he dominates the field not only in his capacity as President of Columbia Artists Management but also in his most cunning ability to sniff out talent. Yet he need not search. They flock to him.

Nothing can be more wrong than to call him an agent. He is a manager in the real and best sense of the word. He is interested in *building* careers. Wilford's first consideration is not only whether the artist is right for the engagement but also whether the engagement is right for the artist, be it for artist development or for a public image. I have seen cases where he urged an artist *not* to accept a well-paid engagement because he did not think it was right for his development at that particular time.

On the other hand, when he achieves an engagement for an artist, this is by no means the end of the matter. He concerns himself with the artist's relationship with the Management and is available at all times with advice. Under his guidance, Columbia is the greatest and most important music agency in the United States. It goes far beyond obtaining engagements for singers and instrumentalists, for opera companies and orchestras. Members of the staff control almost the total inflow of artists and companies from Russia, China—indeed the whole Orient. Wilford's main personal interest is the building of conductors, and through them his influence in the American music world is legitimately enormous. From Ormandy to Ozawa, there are few important conductors who are not under his management.

For any manager, negotiations with artists are one of the most important and difficult tasks.

Every artist needs a different approach. Every artist reacts differently when discussing his demands and wishes.

When the management and the artist are of the same opinion of his or her value, then matters are of course easier. The real problems arise when an artist has a very different view of his value to a company.

At the Met, as elsewhere, it is not always the quality of the voice that determines an artist's value. Of course, there are cases when the voice is so overwhelmingly beautiful that other considerations just might be ignored. But, alas, there are not too many artists whose voices are overwhelming.

Fees, parts, duration of commitment, opening night, new productions, broadcasts—these are only some of the most important issues to settle at the Met and elsewhere. Of course, everything is easier if one can inject a sense of humor. However, not too many artists have a sense of humor. Some artists take themselves so seriously that if you approach them with humor, they take offense. And there are cases that can't be handled with humor—particularly in personal problems.

While I was still at the Met, somebody gave me a little laughing box. I had never seen anything like it before. If one pushed a little button, the box emitted loud human laughter. I used it with artists with whom I had friendly personal contact. So when Corelli came in to ask for a higher fee, unnoticeably to him I activated the little box. It broke the tension and things went more easily thereafter.

Humor is a basic fact of my life.

One of the most difficult discussions concerns roles. It requires great tact to persuade an artist that certain roles successfully sung in the past are no more for him. Very few indeed will admit they may have deteriorated. When a major artist decides to quit, one may regret the departure of a great voice, but at least there is no worry how they will live. Most earn a good deal of money for a long time.

But how does one handle the small comprimario singer who would not have saved anything? Needless to say, there are many more comprimario singers than stars. All the messengers, ladies-in-waiting, Spolettas and Angelottis, for example, have to know twenty or more roles in at least three languages. They have to appear easily three times a week. On occasion, when a star gets sick they must be prepared to jump in and perform a leading role with hardly any rehearsal.

They are the rock on which every opera house is built. Yet hardly anybody knows their names, and they don't draw. For a comprimario singer to advance to a star position, I am sorry to say happens rarely. And that is what makes the difference.

Now comes the time for the comprimario to leave. There the human element makes everything much more difficult. It was naturally difficult for me to write a letter to an artist who had for many years been a loyal member of the Company. Yet I wanted to give the artist ample warning to make plans for the day which inevitably would come.

The type of letter I sent to artists on such occasions would read approximately as follows:

> May I suggest that the time is close when some of us should make way for younger people who are coming up?
>
> I expect in the next two seasons we will try to find a handful of performances for you, but I wonder whether it would not be wise if you would consider retiring from the Metropolitan in two years.
>
> I realize that this letter may upset you, but we all have to recognize the fact that time marches on and try to face it with good grace.
>
> Needless to say, if you wish to discuss the matter further, I shall of course make myself available.

Fortunately, soon after I became General Manager, I simply forced the Board with the help of some enlightened members to start some severance and then some pension arrangement, which helped a lot.

The professional life span of a singer is infinitely shorter than that of business people, who can go on much longer. In many cases you can literally see, or rather hear, the end of a career approaching. Every singer has his or her way of dealing with the inevitable. But, as I said, the artist's financial position plays an important part.

I suggest some form of tax relief for professional singers, realizing that it would be very difficult to find a general solution for everyone. Every singer's circumstances are different. Some are finished at fifty. Others can still sing quite beautifully at sixty. Indeed, it would not be too bad if an age limit were established by the Internal Revenue Service, which would make it easier for young singers to get on.

I was more and more concerned about the desperate position into which the tax situation of foreign singers was driving the Metropolitan. We had some of the most important artists flatly refuse to sign beyond the next season unless the tax situation was cleared up. What they meant by "cleared up" was, among other problems, speedier refunds on overtaxed withholdings.

In addition to negotiations there was always the question of honesty versus diplomacy. Frankly, I tried to combine both. It is hardly possible to enumerate all the thousands of opportunities where a little dishonesty could be used—a change of cast, a sudden call to take over a performance, the shortening of a contract, or the decline of a release or request.

How to handle all these and many more instances depended naturally on the individual artist concerned and also very much on the Manager's personal relationship to the artist. I always felt the outright lie should be avoided under any circumstances. That did not mean that you had to tell a singer that you had heard another singer who you just plainly thought was better. Instead, one could ask if the artist did not feel a little overworked during the week and might one relieve him of this performance. Or, "Did you really feel comfortable in this part? I suspect that the tessitura strained you a bit." Or something of this sort. If nothing worked, one had to come out with the almost naked truth: we wanted to hear Mr. X in this part.

Naturally there were much more complicated issues and it just was not always possible to avoid upsetting a singer. Then one had to weigh his or her upset against the gain of changing the part. This really is closely linked to the whole problem of relationships between Manager and artist.

As I said, I am aware that I was considered "cool" and "aloof." Indeed to a certain extent I think this was true. Yet I felt very much concerned with my staff's personal lives as far as help on my part was concerned. I use the word "staff" because in this consideration, I very much include not only singers but members of the chorus, the ballet, the orchestra and indeed the stagehands. I remember inviting the entire Company rehearsing one day in the old house to come to Sherry's Restaurant and watch the ticker-tape parade for President Kennedy shortly after his inauguration.

I happened to stand next to one of our Italian chorus ladies who had her little daughter with her. When the President came into sight, she told the girl: "Now watch, Kathy. This is President Kennedy and he is the first Catholic President of the United States."

Kathy asked, somewhat surprised, "All the others were Jews?"

I did not make it too easy for anyone to approach me just whenever they liked on any trivial matter or for something there was somebody else they could talk to first.

But I feel sure the Company knew that for any serious personal problem, I would always be available and try to be helpful.

The vicious stories that this was an unhappy House were simply untrue.

Franco Corelli, Nina and Renata Tebaldi when I was awarded the Commander in the Order of Merit of the Republic of Italy. (*credit: Louis Melançon*)

With Mr. and Mrs. Goeran Gentele and Mrs. John Barry Ryan at my last opening night at the Met in 1971. (*credit: Metropolitan Opera Archives*)

With Leontyne Price and Franco Corelli after their joint Met debut in *Trovatore*. (credit: *Louis Melançon*); *Right*, Leonie Rysanek and George London in *Der Fliegende Holländer*. (credit: *Ilse Buhs*)

The morning of my last day in the office holding Herbert von Karajan's telegram. (*credit: Edward Hausner/The New York Times*)

Above, Nina and I entering the opera at the Gala Farewell. Francis Robinson greets us at the left. (*credit: Beth Bergman*); *Far right*, Onstage at my Gala Farewell with some of the artists who performed that evening. (*credit: Metropolitan Opera Archives*)

Birgit Nilsson. (*credit: Sedge LeBlang*)

At last—during one of our morning walks in Suisi.

Discussing the Miami International Festival with my colleague and friend,
Robert Herman. (*credit: Metropolitan Opera Archives*); *Below*, With Beverly Sills at
her last complete opera performance in New York, Menotti's *La Loca*. With us is
John White, for many years the Associate General Manager of the New York
City Opera. (*credit: Beth Bergman*)

In front of Buckingham Palace, the day I became a Knight at the Opera. (*credit: Mugar Memorial Library*)

NINE

ONE OF THE GREAT new inventions that invaded the Met on the opening night of my first season was television. None of us really quite knew what to expect. The influence or effect television would have on opera certainly could not be judged in 1950.

Originally certain managers feared it would have a detrimental effect simply because people would be able to sit in their armchairs at home and not have to pay for their tickets.

Strangely enough, the effect was the opposite. Millions of people became acquainted with an art form they had never enjoyed before. The public got interested and were curious to see opera "live." Television's influence is so enormous that it just cannot be assessed yet.

Think about the telecast of *Elektra*, live from the Met in 1981, with Nilsson and Rysanek heading the cast. It is quite likely that more people may have seen *Elektra* that night than had seen it in all its performances since its premiere in 1909. An awesome thought.

I must confess, I had no idea at that opening-night *Don Carlo* of 1950 just what the future of television and opera might be. What one saw on television in those early days was mostly rotten. It still is. The question for us was how to maintain our standards and yet get into that medium which no doubt was seen by millions. The Met at one period made certain agreements with the CBS network. We presented abbreviated versions of our new productions of *La Bohème* and *Fledermaus* on the then distinguished series *Omnibus*. We also had a series of highlights on the Ed Sullivan show.

At one point Mr. Chotzinoff of NBC called me with a request for an appointment. I asked him to lunch and we had a very pleasant meeting. Mr. Chotzinoff brought up the possibility of the Metropolitan Opera joining with NBC for television opera purposes. It was obvious that he tried to ascertain how "difficult" I would be and how much our basic approaches might differ.

I think he may have left reassured. He was relieved to hear that I wholeheartedly and completely accepted the premise that television opera, even if produced by the Metropolitan, should not emanate from the stage but from a studio. Mr. Chotzinoff was even more relieved to hear that I completely agreed that television opera would have to be in English and that I would not press him to engage certain artists but that casts would have to be photogenic, possibly even at the expense of a little vocal quality.

I did mention to Mr. Chotzinoff that while I considered such collaboration highly desirable, I did feel that the Metropolitan Opera ought to gain substantial economic advantage from it. At any rate, he was aware that we were not thinking of this exclusively in idealistic terms. Mr. Chotzinoff mentioned that of course if a sponsor could be found the economic problem would be infinitely easier, and he admitted that a tie-up with the Metropolitan might facilitate finding sponsors. He seemed not unimpressed with my suggestion of perhaps filling out a program by presenting "great scenes of love and death" or "operatic scenes of vice, horror and ecstasy." For the latter, of course, some of our singers might be indispensable.

🔲🔲

Sorry to say, we never did appear on NBC.

Naturally many of our artists were asked to perform on television. But on occasion one of these appearances would interfere with our schedules.

One artist, much in demand on television, tried to cancel a performance. I wrote:

> I am terribly upset about this business and confess that I resent a little bit your various agents and representatives trying to make it appear once again as if I was the bad boy who, in a bad mood, makes unpleasant decisions. You must know that this is not the case. It would be very much easier for me to say "yes" to all these requests and particularly if they emanate from such attractive young ladies as you are. It would be very much easier, very much more pleasant, and I would just completely fail in my duty to the Metropolitan Opera which, after all, is my first responsibility.
>
> We look upon the Monday performance as an immensely important performance and particularly so for you. It was for that reason that we took you out of another opera on December 22, very reluctantly. It will be inevitable for the subscribers and patrons on the 22nd to be disappointed not to hear you, but this is a risk I was prepared to take in order to save you for Monday. Forgive me if I say that I consider it unfair and unreasonable that instead I am asked to release you to appear the same day, indeed the same hour as our performance is going on, on a widely publicized

television show in New York. How can I justify that to our public? And will your various agents and representatives answer the letters and attacks that will be justly directed against me for such irresponsible planning? I wish you would see it in that light and I am terribly sorry to have to disappoint you. There are not too many singers of your quality around who on top of that are so pretty and so desirable for television and if your various agents would use their energies on the television people rather than on me I think all would be well.

Please don't be angry with me. I hate to do this but I cannot allow my wish to be helpful and my desire to avoid upsetting you cause me to make a decision which would be so clearly against the interests of the Metropolitan Opera.

Naturally the technical developments over the years have been enormous, and that applies particularly to the lighting. When it all started, special lights had to be put in various spots in the auditorium—very much to the discomfort of the audience.

Hardly any of that is necessary anymore. A combination of improved stage lighting with new and very much more sensitive lenses makes that unnecessary.

Even so, there are dark spots on stage. The director has to manage his soloists in such a way that they avoid these spots in important moments.

I do watch the Met telecasts and hear the Met broadcasts. How we all remember the voice of Milton Cross—"the voice of the Met." His announcements during these broadcasts were heard by millions of our listeners for decades. I am sure his name was known by more people than mine and that many thought *he* was running the Met.

The Metropolitan Opera is entrusted with works which it has taken about three hundred years of genius to create. And in relaying these works to the vast audience across America and Canada, Texaco is bringing to millions joy that cannot be measured in terms of surveys or ratings.

I wouldn't be surprised if, in addition to the programs offered to them, children are often introduced to opera by way of television. Having frequently been asked how to get children interested in opera, I wonder if it isn't better, if possible, to introduce opera in an opera house.

To begin with, I would not take them too young. I feel an average child under ten cannot really appreciate opera. I personally have no doubt that *The Magic Flute* is the first opera I would take my child to. Not only will he or she be acquainted with the highest standards of music right from the start, I also feel that the rather naive text can appeal to children. There are the three boys and the animals. There are Pagageno and Papagena—characters that should easily appeal to the young. There is love on a high level.

There is really nothing sad and no force or vulgarity of any kind. In short, I think it is the ideal opera for any child who has any interest in music and wants to go to the opera.

I would wait with Wagner for years. As soon as you move from Mozart, you are apt to run into difficulties with the libretti. Mind you, I am thinking of children of eleven and twelve years of age. Once they get beyond fifteen or so, they can see anything.

I would, at that age, probably start with some Verdi, such as *Rigoletto* or *Aïda* and Puccini's *La Bohème* or *Madama Butterfly*. Naturally *Hansel and Gretel* can always be thrown in if it is in the repertory. If the children have understood and liked them, then they are ready for almost everything—except Wagner.

If eventually Wagner is due, then, I think, stay away from the *Ring* but introduce the romantic operas like *The Flying Dutchman* and *Lohengrin*. Once children hear these and other operas, the way is open. But beware of the *Ring*. Both text and music may destroy anything you have built up.

For the record, *The Magic Flute* is one of my two favorite operas, the other being *Otello*. The opera that I have referred to as my most "unfavorite"—*La Gioconda*.

For the most part I prefer dramatic opera as opposed to most comic ones, as I like confrontation and indeed a sad ending.

While I am impressed with *Salome* and *Elektra*, they both depend on the protagonist. You can enjoy *Der Rosenkavalier* with a partly mediocre cast.

I love almost any Verdi, some Puccini, any Mozart.

I do not care for Stravinsky, even though I recognize his importance.

I seem to like most things and people with style and elegance, which doesn't at all mean elegant dress. It means more style and elegance of behavior.

One night while watching television with Nina, I saw Mayor Koch in short sleeves. Now many people most likely would not mind. Indeed, many may not even have noticed. But it upsets me.

I disapprove of the Mayor of New York City wearing short sleeves in public. I think people in leading positions—private and, even more, public—should lead public behavior and set examples. Just as I prefer a certain code of dress in general.

I am well aware that times and manners have changed. But there must be a limit somewhere.

On many of the television talk shows quite a few so-called "artists" appear in open shirts, without ties. I think that shows a lack of respect for their audience.

In my early days at the Met I would never go

to my box without wearing a tuxedo, and indeed the majority of the audience in boxes or the orchestra would do the same.

However, I remember a Monday night at the Met when, for some reason or another, I didn't change to black tie. A lady, quite well dressed, approached me in the corridor. When she asked me why I wasn't "dressed," I replied: "Madame, if anyone should ask you, just say I don't know."

That has all changed. Within reason I go along with it. But dirty jeans and an open shirt without a tie seems to me to go too far. It is an insult to the artists who try to give their best.

Apart from dress, the general appearance of singers should at least somehow agree with the part they are performing. Alfredo in *La Traviata* and Tamino in *Die Zauberflöte,* just to mention two roles, have to be somewhat believable as youthful lovers or they ruin the story even if the voice is good.

A mezzo-soprano who looks like an elderly fat grandmother simply cannot do Carmen even if the voice is excellent. The parts, and I am not talking about acting, demand a certain illusion without which they cannot be brought off.

As I've stated before, personality is, to me, almost as important as the voice. A beautiful voice without personality leaves me cold and unmoved, while a personality can impress even with a somewhat less outstanding voice but with the tension and excitement that fascinate the listener. One can tell the second a singer walks on stage whether she or he has the indefinable qualities that cannot be learned. The qualities that make a star.

What is personality? It is hard to describe. It is just the effect a person has before doing what they are supposed to do on a stage and subsequently while they are doing it.

A true personality is something that always impresses me, not necessarily only with artists.

Winston Churchill always seemed to me the ultimate of personality. When he entered a room there was nobody else. Callas, too—even without singing. Sir Thomas Beecham—even without conducting. When he mounted the podium, absolute silence descended on the hall before he lifted the baton. Corelli had this quality too in a different way, perhaps because of his glorious appearance in addition to his glorious voice.

On the whole I feel that a singer's private behavior is always inextricably linked with their stage personality. Nobody who saw Callas on stage would imagine her as a warm, cozy person sitting around the fireplace reading a book. Her private personality really was an extension of her stage personality: somewhat cool and distant. No shoulder clapping and quick embrace.

Her movements were slow. She was always impeccably dressed. She never spoke a vulgar word. A "lady" in the best sense of the word. I always said one cannot "search" for a Callas. Such an outstanding figure one can only "find," most likely once or twice in a lifetime—if that.

This brings me to auditions. I cannot even begin to count the many I heard in the course of my professional life. There must have been thousands. To most of these thousands I had to say "thank you" afterward, with nothing following.

Only a fraction were asked, "Please wait." It was a sign of hope when the audition at least warranted a conversation afterward to ascertain the musical background and experience—if any—of the auditioner.

If one looks for a Tosca or a Norma, the judgment both of voice and personality is different from the judgment you apply to a comprimario singer or a young singer who may be trained as a cover.

Auditions are a nervewracking experience for the poor singer who comes out onto an empty stage, looks out into an empty house until he hears a voice from somewhere in the dark asking: "What do you wish to sing?"

I made it a point always to let them sing what they wanted for their first number. And I also always let them sing a second number even if I knew after the first note there was no hope. It's just too humiliating to terminate an audition after the first number.

There are, of course, exceptions. When I engaged Bruno Walter to conduct *Das Lied von der*

Erde at the first Edinburgh Festival, I asked him to come with me to the apartment of some friends in London, where I introduced the then unknown Kathleen Ferrier to him and asked her to sing just a little for him. He listened to just one short song and immediately agreed she should sing in Edinburgh with him. That really introduced her to the world.

Kathleen Ferrier was, no doubt, one of the most outstanding artists of her time. Alas she had only a few more years. She died very young—before I could bring her to the Met for *Orfeo,* which I had planned.

Needless to say, I have followed with interest the careers of those singers who have "made it," and that includes the necessary aids to further their careers. Publicity is such an aid.

The Met has never gone in for creating special publicity for any of its artists. But, of course, individual artists employed their own publicity agents, and what they did was beyond the Met's control unless it assumed such proportion that the Management felt obliged to step in and curb it.

Yet publicity is a very important part of the artistic world and a very difficult one. It is fairly easy to get paid ads in any paper but real publicity is what appears to be unpaid, even though this type of publicity very often costs more.

There is also something called overexposure. At the time of this writing, there is an excellent singer at the Met who, in my view, suffers from overexposure. The publicity manager is getting the name and the not-too-attractive photo into the press via everything from participation in an opera performance, which is legitimate, to events that have nothing to do with the career.

I respect earned publicity. But I don't like the overeager publicity manager who makes one turn the page quickly. Soon one cannot stand one more photo of the artist.

It takes an intelligent manager and, even more so, an intelligent artist, to feel enough is enough. Needless to say, the best publicity is a brilliant performance, when thousands of people go home and tell their friends how much they enjoyed the singer.

Surely it is legitimate to remind the public of one's talents with skill and taste. But not to the extent where the public asks: "My God, does he or she *need* all that publicity?

Sol Hurok understood the value of management and publicity. No book on cultural and artistic life would be complete without his name.

Mr. Hurok was an impressive personality who represented some of the world's finest artists. He was perhaps a shade too powerful as negotiator but we got on well with each other. Many of his singers graced the stage of the Met for years. And to my recollection none suffered the excess publicity I refer to.

TEN

F ORTY YEARS AGO there were no union problems. I realize the present situation is the result of ancient abuses. Much too much time is spent in union negotiations. That time and energy should be conserved to spend on the product, and I, for one, cannot see why we must always be driven to the crisis stage. Some unions are responsible and have leadership with which one can deal openly and fairly and reach equitable agreements in a reasonable time. Others lack leadership and have not attained maturity. They still believe negotiations have to be a battle— a battle which does disservice to both parties, not to mention the public.

It was, of course, a loss not to be able to go to the Met in the fall of 1980 when, once again, there was a long and bitter strike. Once again it was the unions versus the management. If I were active today, I would try to do it differently than I did. We are really in one boat, and we should mutually attempt to prevent the boat from sinking.

When the Met finally opened the 1980–1981 season some three months late, I attended the opening-night performance of *Lulu*. When the opera was first performed at the Met a few years ago, it was the two-act version. On this opening night the complete three-act version was performed with Teresa Stratas in the title role. She gave the performance of her life. Not only was she Lulu, as was to be expected from this extremely talented singing-actress, but she rose to the immense demands vocally, reaching without strain to the top register. It was an amazing performance. In spite of it, I hated the opera.

It was not easy reopening the House in 1969 after a similar strike. When artists are released from their contracts, it is often impossible to reengage them. Looking back, however, I don't think we did too badly that season of 1969–1970.

We opened as late as December 29 with *Aïda*. Price, Dalis, Tucker, and Merrill headed the cast conducted by Molinari-Pradelli. The next night we presented *La Bohème* with Tucci, Gedda, Sereni, Plishka and Corena. Cleva conducted.

Naturally our plans for the season had drastically changed. Luckily we were able to mount our new productions of *Cavalleria Rusticana* and *Pagliacci*. Zeffirelli designed and directed both operas. The singers that evening included Bumbry, Corelli, Guarerra, Amara, Tucker and Milnes with Bernstein conducting *Cav* and Cleva conducting *Pag*.

As for the rest of that quickly-put-together season, we were still able to present *Der Rosenkavalier* in our beautiful production designed by O'Hearn with Boehm conducting and Rysanek, Berry, Ludwig, Popp and Gedda in the leading roles. Boehm also conducted *Der Fliegende Holländer* and *Ariadne auf Naxos* with Rysanek, Grist, Lear, King, Berry and Uppman. *Turandot* was presented with Nilsson and Corelli. And there was a new production of *Norma* designed by Heeley, directed by Deiber, conducted by Bonynge with Sutherland, Horne in her Met debut, Bergonzi and Siepi.

Our two Mozart operas were *Le Nozze di Figaro* and *Die Zauberflöte*. Josef Krips was available to conduct the former with Zylis-Gara, Stratas, Elias, Siepi, Krause and Plishka. The latter had Raskin, Popp, Prey, Gedda, Hines, Dooley and von Stade making her debut as one of the three genii. Stanislaw Skrowaczewski conducted.

Other operas that season were *Traviata, Don Carlo, Madama Butterfly, Fanciulla del West, Roméo et Juliette* and *Andrea Chénier*. In addition we did *Lucia di Lammermoor* and *Carmen* on tour and in our June festival at the Met. Among singers in these operas were Peters, Pilou, Tebaldi, Corelli, Gedda, Kónya, Merrill and Tozzi.

Naturally these artists did not sing all the performances of these operas. But the Met being what it was we were able to cast in other performances such singers as Blegen, Collier, Cossotto, Crespin, Kirsten, Moser, Verrett, Domingo, Edelmann, Gobbi, McCracken and Thomas.

Nevertheless our subscriptions dropped because it appeared New York audiences had got accustomed to living without the Met. It took quite a while to catch up again in these last years of my administration. We never caught up to the full extent. Yet I feel we managed to produce a most respectable season with a number of first-rate artists, only some of whom are mentioned here.

That was also a season when two twenty-fifth anniversaries were observed. Regina Resnik celebrated hers in a performance of *Carmen*. Richard Tucker appeared in an act each of *Aïda*, *Gioconda* and *Traviata*. For this gala occasion he sang with three sopranos—Price, Tebaldi and Sutherland. That was the Met.

ELEVEN

YEARS AGO I WOULD
have a recurring nightmare. Zinka Milanov's spitz,
"Nickie," Maria Callas's poodle, "Toy," and Renata
Tebaldi's poodle, "New," would all advance on me.

"Choose, choose, choose," sang the divas' dogs,
sounding like Alban Berg played backward.

I would wake up screaming.

Actually both Nina and I love dogs—and
Dachshunds in particular. The first we had while
we were in England was a sweet little brown
Dachsy—all three we had were brown and all three
were called Pip after the character in Dickens' *Great
Expectations.* Unfortunately he got sick at a very
young age. At that time some of the medicines they
use today were not available.

We had bad luck with our dogs. Pip II also did

217

not live too long. But Pip III did live for awhile. Then he, too, caught this dreadful disease. We had to put him to sleep. It was a dreadful decision and a heart-breaking farewell. One gets so attached to these little friends. They really become part of one's life.

On one of our trips to Europe we arrived at the airport only to find that the driver of our car refused to take Pip. We dismissed the car and took a cab.

One artist on the Met's national tour always traveled with a dog—and a husband. I received a letter from the hotel manager after their departure. While the manager was honored to have so many stars in his hotel, he noticed that four pillows were missing from this artist's suite. Despite this he would welcome them back next season. However he requested that the dog check in elsewhere.

Of course dogs and other animals are frequently used in opera, including some of the artists'. I recall receiving a telegram from Eleanor Steber informing me that Paco, her wunderhund, had to cancel a performance due to indisposition and on the advice of the dog's psychoanalyst.

Paco received a wire back: "Sorry to hear about your indisposition. Have myself long given up stage performances but look forward to meeting you one of these days" from Pip Bing.

In 1980 I visited my sister Ilka in her home outside of Lisbon. It had been a long time since I traveled without Nina and Pip.

It was a very difficult decision to leave Nina even for only six days. I knew she would be perfectly cared for by our wonderful nurse Mary Fahy.

Yet Nina always misses me, even if I come home late from dinner. My conscience was badly weighed down when I said goodbye. We both were in tears.

I just don't know how anyone can bear traveling these days. Certainly, the jet plane is the greatest enemy of the vocal art. Frankly, just arriving at Kennedy Airport very nearly made me turn around and go home. Seemingly thousands of people were milling around—totally disorganized. There was not a soul to ask for information.

I had a moving and tearful reunion with Ilka. We both had a lot to tell each other.

My beloved sister, a few years older than I, suffers from arthritis and headaches. With a cane and on my arm, we crept around the little square in front of her house enjoying the beautiful weather.

Sometimes during the day I walked alone down to the lovely sea just to run for a little while.

But my thoughts were with Nina—all the time. The distance made it harder. When I telephoned I could, of course, only talk to Mary. But she told me

Nina wanted to hear my voice. She held the receiver to her ear. I said a few words to which Nina could not reply. But Mary said she was all right.

On the trip home I had the horrible idea that Nina might suddenly die and that I would be minutes too late. It became an obsession. But fortunately it was only my dreadful imagination.

When I ran the last steps from the elevator to our door, I found Nina sitting comfortably in her chair. She embraced me with the one arm she can use. We both cried. I happily because she was still with me and I with her.

I did enjoy my days with Ilka. It was just what I had expected—not only love but total understanding and compassion. But what sometimes irritates me a little is that she is so totally on my side. She does not comprehend—indeed she does not wish to comprehend—other people's sufferings.

My life is all she cares for, and only what might help me should be done. It all comes from love— but love only for me. She cannot understand that I would feel much more unhappiness if I left Nina alone. I just cannot turn around and enjoy myself.

It is a strange combination. Ilka can be the kindest and most considerate person. But where her son and I are concerned (there is nobody else of the close family left), she is totally blind to anything but our happiness and welfare—like a lioness defending her cubs.

But it is nice to know there is somebody with this unbounded love ready to sacrifice almost anything to help.

The trip to Portugal was a far cry from the early years when I went on tour with the Met.

In those days we had special trains for the entire company of some three hundred people. The solo artists who didn't wish to sit around flew in and out of the cities. Some had special requests such as cooking facilities. One artist requested a room, large and comfortable and preferably at no charge. Only the scenery went separately. We usually had night trains where, as you can imagine, all sorts of "fun and games" took place. When we arrived at our destination, dozens of buses were waiting to take us to our hotels.

To ensure that the sets arrived on time, we always planned the same opera for the first performance in each city so that the scenery and the costumes could be sent ahead. Naturally, because of the various sizes of the stages, not all the scenery was what was seen in New York. We had, in some cases, special pieces built especially for the tour. Since the tour sponsors pay so much for our performances, it is a pity that conditions don't permit us to show the Met at its best.

I fondly remember the glamorous parties held every opening night in every city. As Nina never traveled with me, I usually took a pretty girl from the ballet as my guest. Even the superstars appeared at these parties.

I would travel back and forth as necessary but Francis Robinson stayed out for the entire tour, much to the delight of the company and the sponsors. Bob Herman was in charge when I was not there.

As for the repertory, I usually picked the popular operas and of course many of our new productions. I always had the best casts we could assemble. The press was usually friendly and polite.

However, years ago, when the Met played Chicago, Claudia Cassidy, then the critic for the *Tribune,* tore us to pieces for five consecutive days—and me in particular. On the sixth day, I met her at the entrance to the theater.

"Oh, Miss Cassidy," I said. "I didn't know you were in town."

I cannot pretend not to be shocked that the State Department, which spent millions sending all kinds of attractions abroad, has not seen fit to show the Metropolitan Opera to another part of the world. The disastrous tour of the Met in Paris was recounted in my first book. The Metropolitan should never have gone small-scale—playing in a small theater with *The Barber of Seville* and *The*

Marriage of Figaro. Sufficient subsidy was impossible. Small-scale is not the Met's style. This unfortunate trip was my fault.

Actually, for some time, the European impresario Leon Leonidoff was attempting to tour the Met in Europe. He requested large-scale works such as *Don Carlo* and *La Forza del Destino* with American artists and those closely associated with the Met such as Zinka Milanov. But without any official subsidy that was obviously impossible.

I think it is nothing short of a national scandal that Leontyne Price should be heard in Russia for the first time with La Scala. She, as well as other distinguished American artists, should have gone to Russia the first time with an American opera company, preferably the Metropolitan.

I miss the tour. It plays a very important role for the Met—then and now.

TWELVE

SEVERAL TIMES each season, the Metropolitan Opera Guild sponsored student matinees. I disapproved of throwing just anything in front of these student audiences. The casts for these performances in my time included major stars as well as younger singers who had the chance to sing major roles. I am happy to say many of these younger singers are singing major roles in many important houses today.

The foundation of the Met's studio, so ably run by John Gutman, did give young singers the chance to try themselves out and gain experience. Yet, for economic reasons, I was wildly against the opera studio. When the studio finally closed, Gutman said in his speech; "My most profound thanks go to Mr. Bing without whose total lack of enthusiasm, this studio couldn't have been possible."

Some years later, when I retired from the Met, it was John who wrote a piece in a special edition of *Opera News* about the "real" me.

While I have tried in this book to reveal something of myself, I frankly admit I wouldn't have thought of his comments. But since they are true, here are some excerpts of that article, reprinted with the kind permission of *Opera News*.

When to the sessions of sweet silent thought I summon up remembrance of Bings past, I am putting his name in the plural intentionally: there have been quite a number of him. And yet, though his image varies often through the decades I have known him, the "basic Rudi" differs little from the original concept.

I first encountered the future knight in Darmstadt, Germany, in the late twenties. He was assistant manager of the opera; it was a good company, and he was *in* good company: Carl Ebert (the boss and stage director), Karl Böhm and Max Rudolf (the conductors). I later asked Ebert whether it was true, as I had often heard, that Bing was a man of habit. Ebert laughed. "That surely is an understatement. In Darmstadt you could go day after day to a certain restaurant, and at 12:48 you would find Rudi Bing at the same corner table, doubtless ordering the same meal."

A man of habit—some will say a slave of habit—he has remained during all the fifty years of his adult life, and if this seems strange in a man whose long career has encompassed four countries and so many way-stations, that is one of the many paradoxes that add up to the figure I now so irreverently call "Sir Rudi." One of his habits is impatience. When I once mentioned this to him, he was not a bit insulted but very much surprised. He was obviously quite unaware that if he asked for a certain task to be carried out, your phone would ring fifteen minutes later and he would inquire if the matter had been taken care of. Once used to this habit, I found it helpful and constructive.

Impatience, I take it, is also at the root of his almost excessive punctuality. Make an appointment with Rudi to go to lunch at 12:45 and you can bet your bottom dollar he will be on your doorstep at 12:41, topcoat, bowler hat, umbrella and all, inquiring plaintively, "Aren't we going to lunch?"

But now let us advance the date to November 3, 1949. The scene: the pier on which Nina and Rudi landed. . . . Talking of habit, they moved into a suite at the Essex House, and that is where they still live today. We escorted them to their royal home and then went to dinner together. Rudi asked me to join him at the Met, and since then—for twenty-two hectic, often exhilarating years—we have hardly ever been separable, except for summer vacations and weekends. Friendship or no, how much closer can you get to a man than living door to door with him eight or twelve hours a day? In the old opera house, my desk was so close to his door that I could open it without getting up from my chair.

Who is he—Rudolf Bing, Mr. Bing, Bing, Sir Rudolf, Rudi? He is, obviously, all of them. Will the real Rudi please stand up? No, he won't. I don't think he exists. To begin with, there is an infinity of difference between the true being of any man and his public image. Few realize, I believe, the tremendous difference between Rudi the man and Sir Rudolf the image. I do not divulge any secrets, nor do I fear to offend Rudi, if I say that his image often has not been exactly flattering, that it is full of shadows. He has largely, often artificially, created that image and, I suspect, enjoyed it enormously. A martinet, a dictator, a soulless wooden statue of himself: if he has ever resented any of these epithets, he has not shown it. A great queen of the American theater was once introduced in London to an English lady with the remark, "You will be glad to meet one of the friends of Rudolf Bing." "Ah, really," retorted the American, "I did not know he had any." To stay on the British side for a moment, Cyril Ritchard once said, "Don't be misled—behind that cold, austere, severe exterior, there beats a heart of stone." The American in London spoke in malicious earnest; Cyril was affectionatly slanderous. He was a friend.

If you turned the pages of the twenty-two-year history book of the Bing regime, you'd find far fewer "scandals" than you'd like to remember, and if you viewed them from the disadvantage point of the general manager you'd agree that he frequently had to do what he did. . . .

I have often wondered what an outsider, preferably an inimical one, would think of a staff meeting in Rudi's office. If the quality of a management could be determined by the number of laughs studding such a meeting, ours must have been a pretty good one. . . .

Rudi's sense of humor is less well known than his wit, which not infrequently was frightening in its bite.

Those twenty-two years at the Met have been the mainstay of his life. Years ago a San Francisco reporter asked me what counted most in Bing's life away from the opera house. I said his dog and his wife, in that order. The utter devotion of both Bings to Pip, the dachshund (by now the third of the dynasty), is well-nigh incomprehensible to any but the most devout dog-lover. Except for Sir Rudi's brief recent trip to accept knighthood, they have not been in England, their beloved adoptive country, in almost twenty years. The reason: Pip cannot enter, because of the quarantine laws. Would you trust your eyes if one gray, drizzly morning about seven you saw the general manager of the Metropolitan Opera, in pajamas and slippers, guiding Pip on his early constitutional? Do take my word for it. And how about this: early in the 1950's, soon after the new regime started, in the middle of a morning meeting in Bing's office he suddenly looked at his watch, excused himself, asked his colleagues to continue, put on coat and hat and disappeared, to return forty minutes later. What had happened? Mrs. Bing was ill, and who was to take Pip for his 11:30 walk? A servant? A maid? An elevator boy? Not on your life!

Unbelievable? Yet it fits so well into the picture, because it does not fit the image at all. Nor does his complete contempt for "glamour." True, Rudi did not hide his pleasure in becoming Sir Rudolf, and his box at the Met was always full of ambassadors and the like, but anyone who claims to have seen Bing's name frequently in a society column must be an avid reader. . . .

Finally, the "heart of stone." I fear at this late date it would be futile to attempt to change the image of the statue of the Commendatore on his high horse. All too few know the Rudi that is hiding in Sir Rudolf. He, by the way, would not agree that they are all too few, and would be content to have his true heart stay in hiding. If his extraordinary composure in professional situations has stood him in good stead, it has quite naturally contributed to the legend of the man for all opera seasons but a ghost outside them. If so, he is surely the kindest ghost I have ever met. I, who know that a good part of his arrogance is attributable to his need not to admit a basic shyness, also know he can be emotional to the point of being sentimental.

To reveal instances of the human and humane Bing would mean entering the forbidden domain of privacy, but let me end on a personal note that I think will illustrate the cardiac analysis of the then not yet Sir Rudolf.

Late in December 1937 a German singer friend, Rose Walter, gave my wife and me a farewell party, giving us up for lost because we were presently to emigrate to that dark continent America. Rudi was there; so was Nina; and so was a young Austrian soprano, who offered one of those popular Viennese songs which your mind's ear recognizes as an illegitimate attack on your tear ducts but which at the same time prove what somebody once called the emotional powers of bad music. Here is what the song said: *"Sag beim Abschied leise 'servus'—nicht goodby und nicht adieu; diese Worte tun mir weh. . . ."*

"Servus," of course, is Latin for "slave." In Hungary or Vienna, when two friends meet casually and part casually they greet each other with *"servus,"* originally meaning, I take it, "I am your obedient servant," today meaning no more than a fond "so long." The song in English: "When we part, say softly 'servus'—not goodbye and not adieu, for these words would hurt too much."

Early January of the year 1938 found my wife and me in Paris, casting a long, nostalgic glance at dear old Europe and all excited about joining the melting pot. The eve of our departure, we were feverishly packing our not too numerous belongings when a telegram appeared under the door of our hotel room. It read, *"Sag beim Abschied leise 'servus.'"* I suppose I need not mention the sender's name.

Servus, Rudi.

As I have said, I don't believe the Met was an unhappy House during my regime. Indeed I was delighted to receive a telegram from the Met Orchestra when I was knighted.

It read: "Congratulations on the well-deserved honor bestowed upon you by Her Majesty Queen Elizabeth."

I wonder which is the greater honor: the knighthood or the recognition of this splendid orchestra.

🔲🔲

No major opera house can successfully run a season without a number of prominent and internationally known artists, preferably American. The Met had its share in my time. But not all great artists get along with each other.

When we were planning the *Ring* with Karajan as director and conductor, it became evident that there was a problem with Birgit Nilsson. She wrote to me that she didn't want to be the cause of preventing Karajan from direcing his *Ring*. She commented that it was kind of me to choose her before Karajan. She then added: "I would choose you before him too."

But there were problems I simply did not know how to resolve.

The wife of one of our leading tenors wrote that two days before *Otello* her husband was too nervous. Two days after Otello, he was too tired. She pleaded: "Where does that leave me when you schedule *Otello* twice in one week."

Singers have every right to be nervous. Every

time the curtain rises their lives are at stake. Every sour note at the Met is discussed the next day at La Scala.

Some of our younger singers would ask for recommendations for singing teachers. There was a firm policy that the Met Management would not recommend individual singing teachers.

The reason was simply that one teacher might achieve fabulous results with one singer while his or her methods might ruin another singer. The Met Management could not be put in the position of deciding who was good for one pair of vocal cords and who wasn't.

I have no negative thoughts about the new Met. As I began my eighth season in 1957, Harold Schonberg interviewed me on my "dream" opera house. I remember I asked for the stage equipment of Cologne, the sweeping foyers of Paris and a red and gold interior with the acoustics of La Scala. I think we have them as close as you are ever going to have them in the new Metropolitan Opera House in Lincoln Center.

There were many who made this house and indeed Lincoln Center possible. One was Mr. John D. Rockefeller III. I remember one evening when Nina and I had dinner with him. Nina turned and asked: "And what do *you* do, Mr. Rockefeller?" I don't know to this moment what the poor man answered. My darling wife was totally unimpressed with social standing or money.

I cannot end this book without mentioning two very special friends: Nin Ryan and Peggy Douglas. Quite apart from their membership on the Board of Directors, they were and are real personal friends to whom I am grateful for long-lasting and loyal friendship.

I am grateful to the thousands who were employed at the Met during my tenure.

And I am grateful to Ronald Wilford. I don't know what would have happened to me if he had not offered his helping hand.

I hope I brought the Met into the twentieth century—which was only a rumor when I came. I paired such directors as Webster, Kanin, Lunt, Barrault, Brook and Zeffirelli with designers like Chagall, Berman, Gérard, Beaton, Messel and Zeffirelli.

I would have been more adventurous if I had been at Hamburg where the state pays. Here I felt my job was to keep the place open.

A reporter once asked if I was anti-German or pro-Italian opera. I answered: "I am neither pro-German nor pro-Italian—I am pro good opera! I will admit that my natural inclination is rather toward the Italian wing but I have not produced opera to please myself but to please the public."

There is a difference between becoming famous and becoming controversial. I became controversial and enjoyed it. I was never anxious to be peaceful.

APPENDIX I

T HE FOLLOWING LIST
of conductors, singers, dancers and choreographers represents the total artistic roster during my tenure of twenty-two years. Directors and designers are listed under the new productions.

While every effort has been made to insure a complete listing, it may be possible that inadvertently one or the other name may have been left out, which indeed if it is the case is deeply regretted.

Whether one or the other artist appeared once or many times could not be distinguished in this list.

CONDUCTORS

Claudio Abbado
Kurt Adler
Franz Allers
Bruno Amaducci
Ernest Ansermet
Ernesto Barbini
Serge Baudo
Jan Behr
Leonard Bernstein
Josef Blatt
Karl Boehm
Richard Bonynge
Julius Burger
Renato Cellini
Pietro Cimara
Fausto Cleva

Colin Davis
Christoph von
 Dohnanyi
Alberto Erede
Carlo Franci
Lamberto Gardelli
Raymond Gniewek
Walter Hagen
Herbert von Karajan
Christopher Keene
Rudolf Kempe
Berislav Klobucar
Tibor Kozma
Josef Krips
Robert La Marchina
Erich Leinsdorf

James Levine
Alain Lombard
Leopold Ludwig
Lorin Maazel
Zubin Mehta
Dimitri Mitropoulos
Francesco Molinari-
  Pradelli
Pierre Monteux
Jean Morel
Eugene Ormandy
Gabor Otvös
Georges Prêtre
John Pritchard
Fritz Reiner
Martin Rich
Joseph Rosenstock
Max Rudolf

Nello Santi
George Schick
Thomas Schippers
Stanislaw
  Skrowaczewski
Sir George Solti
William Steinberg
Fritz Stiedry
Leopold Stokowski
Ignace Strasfogel
George Szell
Walter Taussig
Victor Trucco
Silvio Varviso
Michelangelo Veltri
Nino Verchi
Hans Wallat
Bruno Walter

SINGERS

Karola Agai
Licia Albanese
Mildred Allen
Jeannine Altmeyer
Lucine Amara
Belen Amparan
Marian Anderson
Karan Armstrong
Martina Arroyo
Elizabeth Anguish*

Radmila Bakocevic
Marcia Baldwin
Fedora Barbieri
Klara Barlow
Teresa Berganza
Erna Berger
Maria Bieshu

Ingrid Bjoner
Lynn Blair
Judith Blegen
Colette Boky
Anne Bollinger
Inge Borkh
Beverly Bower
Karin Branzell
Nadyne Brewer
Phyllis Brill
Lucielle Browning
Grace Bumbry
Patricia Berlin*
Ada Brysac*
Rose Byrum*

Montserrat Caballé
Maria Callas
Kitty Carlisle
Clarice Carson

*Chorus.

244

Nedda Casei
Laura Castellano
Elena Cernei
Madelaine Chambers
Lili Chookasian
Joy Clements
Marie Collier
Nadine Conner
Viorica Cortez
Fiorenza Cossotto
Mary Costa
Dorothy Coulter
Régine Crespin
Gilda Cruz-Romo
Emilia Cundari
Phyllis Curtin
Mary Curtis-Verna
Biserka Cvejic
Ada Calabrese*
Rae Calitri*
Charleen Clark*
Patricia Clarke*
Madelyn Coppock*

Irene Dalis
Gianna d'Angelo
Gloria Davy
Ina Delcampo

Lisa Della Casa
Victoria
   De Los Angeles
Judith De Paul
Christina Deutekom
Loretta di Franco
Mattiwilda Dobbs
Mignon Dunn
Ludmila Dvorakova
Evangeline
   De Florio*
Dina de Salvo*
Constance
   Di Giacomo*

Rosalind Elias
Barbro Ericson
Cecelia Entner*
Ella Eure*

Eileen Farrell
Jean Fenn
Kirsten Flagstad
Judith Forst
Mirella Freni
Mary Fercana*
Nora Feurstein*
Ann Florio*

*Chorus.

Vilma Georgiou
Herta Glaz
Batyah Godfrey
Christel Goltz
Rita Gorr
Maria Gray
Joann Grillo
Reri Grist
Elisabeth Grümmer
Hilde Gueden
Ethel Greene*

Margaret Harshaw
Hildegard
   Hillebrecht
Elisabeth Hoengen
Grace Hoffman
Marilyn Horne
Lois Hunt
Rosalind Hupp
Laurel Hurley
Elinor Harper*
Elizabeth Holiday*
Florence Holland*

Kunie Imai

Gundula Janowitz

Maria Jeritza
Irene Jessner
Junetta Jones
Irene Jordan
Alexandra (Lexi)
   Jones*

Raina Kabaivanska
Lucille Kailer
Margaret Kalil
Gwendolyn Killebrew
Dorothy Kirsten
Maria Kouba
Jean Kraft
Heidi Krall
Gladys Kriese
Gladys Kuchta
Lorraine Keane*
Jane Kirwan*

Gerda Lammers
Evelyn Lear
Paula Lenchner
Maria Leone
Brenda Lewis
Caterina Ligendza
Gloria Lind
Marion Lippert

*Chorus.

Martha Lipton
Aase Nordmo
   Loevberg
Pilar Lorengar
Shirley Love
Christa Ludwig
Ruth Lansché*
Gladys Lansing*
Gail Leonard*
Edna Lind*
Elyssa Lindner*

Mary MacKenzie
Virginia MacWatters
Jean Madeira
Luisa Malagrida
Adriana Maliponte
Simone Mangelsdorff
Janis Martin
Edith Mathis
Johanna Meier
Jolanda Meneguezzer
Kerstin Meyer
Zinka Milanov
Mildred Miller
Martha Moedl
Anna Moffo
Mariquita Moll

Edda Moser
Patrice Munsel
Ivanka Myhal
Jean Melatti*
Helen McIlhenny*
Pamela Munson*

Maria Nache
Herva Nelli
Elena Nikolaidi
Birgit Nilsson
Maralin Niska
Betsy Norden
Jarmila Novotna

Joyce Olson
Carlotta Ordassy
Rita Orlandi
Lynn Owen

Jeanne Palmer
Nicoletta Panni
Claudia Parada
Janet Pavek
Louise Pearl
Roberta Peters
Marguerite Piazza
Helga Pilarczyk

*Chorus.

Jeanette Pilou
Marcella Pobbe
Lily Pons
Lucia Popp
Ruza Pospinov
   (Ruza Baldani)
Mary Ellen Pracht
Leontyne Price
Meredith Parsons*
Alice Plotkin†
Raeschelle Potter*
Lisa Puleo*

Nell Rankin
Judith Raskin
Lillian Raymondi
Liselotte Rebmann
Regina Resnik
Anna Reynolds
Jane Rhodes
Delia Rigal
Graciela Rivera
Margherita Roberti
Francesca Roberto
Gail Robinson
Margaret Roggero
Elinor Ross

Anneliese
   Rothenberger
Leonie Rysanek
Nancy Reep*

Nerina Santini
Bidu Sayao
Eileen Schauler
Marianne Schech
Ursula Schröder
   (Ursula Schröder-
   Feinen)
Elisabeth
   Schwarzkopf
Renata Scotto
Jeanette Scovotti
Irmgard Seefried
Anja Silja
Giulietta Simionato
Monica Sinclair
Elisabeth
   Soederstroem
Frederica von Stade
Eleanor Steber
Antonietta Stella
Risë Stevens
Teresa Stich-Randall

*Chorus.
†Child singer.

Milka Stojanovic
Teresa Stratas
Lilian Sukis
Joan Sutherland
Dina Salvo*
May Savage*
Judit Schichtanz*
Celeste Scott*
Dorothy Shawn*
Lilias Sims*

Renata Tebaldi
Blanche Thebom
Neyde Thomaz
Hertha Töpper
Georgetta Toth
Helen Traubel
Barbara Troxell
Gabriella Tucci
Norma Taubert*

Anita Välkki
Helen Vanni
Astrid Varnay
Shakeh Vartenissian
Josephine Veasey
Shirley Verrett
Galina Vishnevskaya

Thelma Votipka
Athena Vicos*

Joan Wall
Sandra Warfield
Genevieve Warner
Felicia Weathers
Walburga Wegner
Ljuba Welitch
Patricia Welting
Carol Wilcox
Nancy Williams
Dolores Wilson
Nadja Witkowska

Francis Yeend
Maria Yauger*

Hilde Zadek
Virginia Zeani
Teresa Zylis-Gara

GENTLEMEN

Theo Adam
Bernd Aldenhoff
John Alexander
Luigi Alva

*Chorus.

249

Lorenzo Alvary
Charles Anthony
Giacomo Aragall
Erbert Aldridge*
Gene Allen*
John Allan*
Max Alperstein*
Joseph Andreacchi*
Henry Arthur*

Salvatore Baccaloni
Gabriel Bacquier
John Baker
Cesare Bardelli
Gaetano Bardini
Daniele Barioni
Ettore Bastianini
Kurt Baum
Carlo Bergonzi
Walter Berry
Richard Best
Jussi Bjoerling
Sigurd Bjoerling
Kurt Boehme
Franco Bonisolli
Kim Borg
Umberto Borso
Pietro Bottazzo

Ron Bottcher
Gene Boucher
Algerd Brazis
Helge Brilioth
John Brownlee
Renato Bruson
Arthur Budney
Stuart Burrows
Ion Buzea
Arthur Backgren*
Anthony Balestrieri*
Nicola Barbusci*
Etienne Barone*
Erich Birlenbach*
John Bogart*
John Budney*
Ludwig Burgstaller*
Peter Burke*

Giuseppe Campora
Renato Capecchi
Piero Cappuccilli
Gabor Carelli
Mariano Caruso
Walter Cassel
Richard Cassilly
Nico Castel
George Cehanovsky

*Chorus.

250

Leslie Chabay
Russell Christopher
Renato Cioni
William Cochran
Anselmo Colzani
Eugene Conley
Franco Corelli
Fernando Corena
Dominic Cossa
Jon Crain
Oskar Czerwenka
Gerald Carpenter*
Vladimir Chistiakov*
Frank Coffey*
Charles Cooke*
Thomas Cooke*
Guy Curtis*

Albert Da Costa
Emery Darcy
Lawrence Davidson
Leonard Del Ferro
Mario Del Monaco
Alessio De Paolis
Justino Diaz
Murray Dickie
Enrico Di Giuseppe
Giuseppe Di Stefano

Nicholas Di Virgilio
Andrij Dobriansky
Karl Doench
Placido Domingo
William Dooley
Loren Driscoll
John Robert Dunlap
Luigi De Cesare*
Frank D'Elia*
William Dembaugh*
Paul De Paola*

Otto Edelmann
Dezso Ernster
Elfego Esparza
Geraint Evans
Darwin Emanuel*

Sebastian Feiersinger
Gerd Feldhoff
Eugenio Fernandi
Agostino Ferrin
Ezio Flagello
Herbert Fliether
Dino Formichini
Paul Franke
Ferdinand Frantz
Gottlob Frick

*Chorus.

251

Matthew Farruggio*
Emil Filip*
Gary Finkelstein*
Alan Fischer†
Stuart Fischer†
Joseph Folmer*
Luis Forero*
John Frydel*

Josef Gabriels
Giulio Gari
Nicolai Gedda
Nicolai Ghiaurov
Franco Ghitti
Nicola Ghiuselev
Bonaldo Giaiotti
Raymond Gibbs
Giovanni Gibin
Gary Glaze
Peter Glossop
Tito Gobbi
Leo Goeke
Robert Goodloe
Igor Gorin
Arthur Graham
Donald Gramm
Josef Greindl

Donald Grobe
Frank Guarrera
Giangiacomo Guelfi
Edward Ghazal*
Norman Giffin*

Mack Harrell
Clifford Harvuot
Osie Hawkins
Thomas Hayward
Joshua Hecht
Ralph Herbert
Nicolae Herlea
Jerome Hines
Richard Holm
Hans Hopf
Hans Hotter
Edmond Hurshell
Gerard Harrington*
Walter Hemmerly*
Peter Herzberg*
Orrin Hill*

Herbert Janssen
David Johnson*

Edmond Karlsrud

*Chorus.
†Child singer.

Zoltan Kelemen
Norman Kelley
James King
Peter Klein
Rudolf Knoll
Sándor Kónya
Endre Koreh
Alfredo Kraus
Tom Krause
Fritz Krenn
Paul Kuen
Charles Kullman
Erich Kunz
Benno Kusche
Kris Kalfayan †
George Keith †
Kurt Kessler *
Arnold Kirschberg *
Adam Klein †
Arnold Knight *
Charles Kuestner *

Flaviano Labo
Theodore Lambrinos
Bruno Landi
Michael Langdon
Pedro Lavirgen

Virgilio Lazzari
William Lewis
Karl Liebl
Pavel Lisitsian
George London
Ermanno Lorenzi
Kevin Leftwich *

James McCracken
Barry McDaniel
Robert McFerrin
Andrew McKinley
Cornell MacNeil
Rod MacWherter
John Macurdy
Matteo Manuguerra
Dan Marek
Calvin Marsh
Morley Meredith
Robert Merrill
Josef Metternich
Raymond Michalski
Sherrill Milnes
Norman Mittelmann
Barry Morell
James Morris
Nicola Moscona

*Chorus.
†Child singer.

William McLuckey*
René Mack*
Frank Mandile*
Lou Marcella*
Herman Marcus*
Peter Mark†
Paul Marko*
Rudolf Mayreder*
William Mellow*
Roland Miles*
Giulio Mollica*
Fawayne Murphy*

Octaviano Naghiu
Robert Nagy
Nikola Nikolov
Sven Nilsson
Pekka Nuotio

William Olvis
Aurelio Oppicelli
Mario Ortica

Ticho Parly
Kostas Paskalis
Robert Patterson
Luciano Pavarotti

Gerhard Pechner
Jan Peerce
Gino Penno
Alois Pernerstorfer
Sergio Pezzetti
Ion Piso
Paul Plishka
Gianni Poggi
Abe Polakoff
Giacinto Prandelli
Bruno Prevedi
Hermann Prey
Thomas Powell*
Robert Puleo†

Louis Quilico

Gianni Raimondi
Ruggero Raimondi
John Reardon
Roald Reitan
Karl Ridderbusch
Nicola Rossi-Lemeni
Marko Rothmuller
Vladimir Ruzdak
Earl Ringland*
Hal Roberts*

*Chorus.
†Child singer.

George Ryan †

Lorenzo Saccomani
Robert Schmorr
Paul Schoeffler
Kenneth Schon
Norman Scott
Peter Schreier
Mario Sereni
Arturo Sergi
Louis Sgarro
George Shirley
Cesare Siepi
Paolo Silveri
Leopold Simoneau
Martial Singher
Kenneth Smith
Enzo Sordello
Gérard Souzay
Ludovic Spiess
Thomas Stewart
Gerhard Stolze
Brian Sullivan
Set Svanholm
Randolph Symonette
Bruce Scott *
Harry Shean *

Peter Sliker *
Lloyd Stang *
William Stanz *
William Starling *
Harold Sternberg *
Sam Sternberg *
Andrew Strasfogel †

Ferruccio Tagliavini
Franco Tagliavini
Martti Talvela
Lorenzo Testi
Jess Thomas
Hugh Thompson
Giorgio Tozzi
Günther Treptow
Richard Tucker
John Tyers
Carlo Tomanelli *
John Trehy *

Hermann Uhde
Theodor Uppman
Dimiter Uzunov

Giuseppe Valdengo
Frank Valentino

*Chorus.
†Child singer.

Cesare Valletti
Andrea Velis
Richard Verreau
Luben Vichey
  (Lubomir
    Vichegonov)
Jon Vickers
Ramon Vinay
Ivo Vinco

Eberhard Wächter
William Walker
David Ward

Leonard Warren
Robert Weede
Ernst Wiemann
Otto Wiener
William Wilderman
Wolfgang
  Windgassen
Benjamin Wilkes*

Primo Zambruno
Giuseppe Zampieri
Mario Zanasi
William Zakariasen*

*Chorus.

ACTORS

Michael Ebert
Jack Gilford
Gilbert Ireland
Alfred Lunt

Jack Mann
Cyril Ritchard
Walter Slezak

CHOREOGRAPHERS

Alvin Ailey
Thomas Andrew
Todd Bolender
Hans Brenaa
William Burdick
John Butler
Alexandra Danilova
Lele De Triana
Katherine Dunham
Flemming Flindt
Mattlyn Gavers

Dania Krapska
Yurik Lazowski
Alicia Markova
Matt Mattoy
Cyril Ritchard
Donald Saddler
Zachary Solov
Milko Sparemblek
John Taras
Antony Tudor

DANCERS

Wally Adams
Ivan Allen
Jacques d'Amboise
Suzanne Ames
Thomas Andrew
Anna Aragno
Madeleine Artieres
Suzanne Aschieu
Micheline Bardin
Pina Bausch
Socrates Birsky
Robert Bishop
Margaret Black
Ingrid Blecker
Larry Boyette
Sally Brayley

Oleg Briansky
William Burdock
Edward Caton
Frances Cavicchio
Judith Chazin
Eugene Collins
Janet Collins
Rex Cooper
Craig Crosson
Cathryn Damon
Robert Davis
Carmen DeLavallade
Scott Douglas
Laurence Eddington
Miriam Ehrenberg
Nicolyn Emanuel

Thomas Enckell
Ann Etgar
Skiles Fairlie
Hubert Farrington
Edilio Ferraro
Martin Friedman
Nana Gollner
Josef Gregory
Sylvia Grinvald
Natalie Grishin
Jose Gutierrez
Melissa Hayden
Patricia Heyes
Loren Hightower
Jane Hillyer
Ilona Hirschl
Geoffrey Holder
Catherine Horn
Kathyrn Horne
Marion Horosko
Edith Jerrell
Harry Jones
Rhodie Jorgenson
Gloria Kapilow
Maria Karnilova
Louis Kasman
Audrey Keane
Natalie Kelepovska
Nancy King
Karl Klausen

Pauline Knitzer
Vittorio Korjhan
Carole Kroon
Pierre Lacotte
Yurek Lazowski
Sandra Lee
Diana Levy
Bambi Linn
Christopher Lyall
Gloria Lyons
Malcolm McCormick
Fern MacLarnon
Donald Mahler
Viola Maiorca
William Maloney
Lynn Marcus
Alicia Markova
Bruce Marks
Naomi Marritt
Carolyn Martin
Donald Martin
Michael Maule
Hans Meister
Medanya Michalie
Jan Mickens
David Milnes
Arthur Mitchell
Janet Morse
Tilda Morse
Mary Ellen Moylan

Ron Murray
Zebra Nevins
John Nola
Sharon O'Connell
Nira Paez
Adelino Palomanos
Franz Piper
Ali Pourfarrokh
Gilbert Reed
Thomas Russell
Lolita San Miguel
Anthony Santiago
Peter Saul
Howard Sayette
Jean Lee Schock
Ron Sequoio
Lupe Serrano
Louellen Sibley
Mia Slavenska

Eugene Slavin
Peggy Smithers
Khemfoia Tol Padu
Diana Turner
Roland Vasquez
Violette Verdy
Adriano Vitale
Marsha Warren
Lance Westergard
Steve Wiland
Joan Wilder
Kenlin Wilder
Lee Wilson
Sallie Wilson
Franklin Yeger
Judith Younger
Igor Youskevitch
Richard Zelens

APPENDIX II

REPERTORY

THE FOLLOWING is the repertory produced during my tenure, with the number of seasons and performances each work received.

	SEASONS	PERFOR-MANCES
Adriana Lecouvreur	2	23
Aïda	20	198
Alcestis	2	12
Andrea Chénier	8	59
Antony and Cleopatra	1	8
Arabella	4	22
Ariadne auf Naxos	3	20
Un Ballo in Maschera	9	62
Il Barbiere di Siviglia	8	75
La Bohème	18	202

	SEASONS	PERFOR-MANCES
Boris Godunov	6	41
Carmen	15	154
Cavalleria Rusticana	13	105
Les Contes d'Hoffmann	6	43
Così Fan Tutte	7	47
Don Carlo	12	73
Don Giovanni	14	115
Don Pasquale	4	25
Elektra	6	28
L'Elisir d'Amore	5	43
Ernani	4	25
Eugene Onegin	3	20
Falstaff	5	44
La Fanciulla del West	3	30
Faust	11	107
Fidelio	6	50
La Fille du Régiment	1	11
Die Fledermaus	10	70
Der Fliegende Holländer	6	62
La Forza del Destino	9	77
Die Frau ohne Schatten	3	23
Der Freischütz	1	9
Gianni Schicchi	2	11
La Gioconda	8	56
Götterdämmerung	5	20
The Gypsy Baron	1	9
Hansel and Gretel	2	17
The Last Savage	2	10
Lohengrin	7	50
Lucia di Lammermoor	13	110
Luisa Miller	2	19
Macbeth	4	23

Madama Butterfly	18	147
Manon	5	33
Manon Lescaut	6	39
Martha	2	14
Die Meistersinger	12	77
Mourning Becomes Electra	2	11
Nabucco	1	9
Norma	4	29
Le Nozze di Figaro	13	93
Orfeo ed Euridice	4	25
Otello	9	65
Pagliacci	13	105
Parsifal	12	40
Pelléas et Mélisande	4	22
La Périchole	5	37
Peter Grimes	2	13
Queen of Spades	2	16
The Rake's Progress	2	7
Verdi *Requiem*	3	6
Das Rheingold	4	13
Rigoletto	15	139
Roméo et Juliette	3	29
Der Rosenkavalier	9	71
Salome	7	44
Samson et Dalila	6	41
Siegfried	3	9
Simon Boccanegra	4	29
La Sonnambula	3	30
Tannhäuser	4	23
Tosca	16	183
La Traviata	17	179
Tristan und Isolde	9	55
Il Trovatore	12	108
Turandot	7	63

Vanessa	3	15
Die Walküre	9	43
Werther	2	18
Wozzeck	4	18
Die Zauberflöte	8	70
Galas	15	19

NEW PRODUCTIONS*

1950–51:

Don Carlo (Verdi): designed by Rolf Gérard, staged by Margaret Webster, conducted by Fritz Stiedry

Der Fliegende Holländer (Wagner): designed by Charles Elson, after Robert Edmond Jones and Mary Percy Schenck, staged by Herbert Graf, conducted by Fritz Reiner

Fledermaus (J. Strauss): designed by Rolf Gérard, staged by Garson Kanin, conducted by Eugene Ormandy

Cavalleria Rusticana (Mascagni): designed by Horace Armistead, staged by Hans Busch, conducted by Alberto Erede

Pagliacci (Leoncavallo): designed by Horace Armistead, staged by Max Leavitt, conducted by Alberto Erede

*This list is provided courtesy of *Opera News*.

1951–52:

Aïda (Verdi): designed by Rolf Gérard, staged by Margaret Webster, conducted by Fausto Cleva

Rigoletto (Verdi): designed by Eugene Berman, staged by Herbert Graf, conducted by Alberto Erede

Così Fan Tutte (Mozart): designed by Rolf Gérard, staged by Alfred Lunt, conducted by Fritz Stiedry

Carmen (Bizet): designed by Rolf Gérard, staged by Tyrone Guthrie, conducted by Fritz Reiner

1952–53:

La Forza del Destino (Verdi): designed by Eugene Berman, staged by Herbert Graf, conducted by Fritz Stiedry

La Bohème (Puccini): designed by Rolf Gérard, staged by Joseph L. Mankiewicz, conducted by Alberto Erede

The Rake's Progress (Stravinsky): designed by Horace Armistead, staged by George Balanchine, conducted by Fritz Reiner

1953–54:

Faust (Gounod): designed by Rolf Gérard, staged by Peter Brook, conducted by Pierre Monteux

Tannhäuser (Wagner): designed by Rolf Gérard, staged by Herbert Graf, conducted by George Szell

Il Barbiere di Siviglia (Rossini): designed by Eugene Berman, staged by Cyril Ritchard, conducted by Alberto Erede

1954–55:

Andrea Chénier (Giordano): designed by Frederick Fox, staged by Dino Yannopoulos, conducted by Fausto Cleva

Vittorio (Verdi): designed by Esteban Frances, choreography by Zachary Solov, conducted by Dimitri Mitropoulos

Arabella (R. Strauss): designed by Rolf Gérard, staged by Herbert Graf, conducted by Rudolf Kempe

1955–56:

Les Contes d'Hoffmann (Offenbach): designed by Rolf Gérard, staged by Cyril Ritchard, conducted by Pierre Monteux

Soirée (Rossini-Britten): designed by Cecil Beaton, choreography by Zachary Solov, conducted by Thomas Schippers

Don Pasquale (Donizetti): designed by Wolfgang Roth, staged by Dino Yannopoulos, conducted by Thomas Schippers

The Magic Flute (Mozart): designed by Harry Horner, staged by Herbert Graf, conducted by Bruno Walter

1956–57:

Ernani (Verdi): designed by Esteban Frances, staged by Dino Yannopoulos, conducted by Dimitri Mitropoulos

La Périchole (Offenbach): designed by Rolf Gérard, staged by Cyril Ritchard, conducted by Jean Morel

La Traviata (Verdi): designed by Oliver Smith and Rolf Gérard, staged by Tyrone Guthrie, conducted by Fausto Cleva

1957–58:

Eugene Onegin (Tchaikovsky): designed by Rolf Gérard,

staged by Peter Brook, conducted by Dimitri Mitropoulos

Don Giovanni (Mozart): designed by Eugene Berman, staged by Herbert Graf, conducted by Karl Boehm

Vanessa (Barber): designed by Cecil Beaton, staged by Gian Carlo Menotti, conducted by Dimitri Mitropoulos

Madama Butterfly (Puccini): designed by Motohiro Nagasaka, staged by Yoshio Aoyama, conducted by Dimitri Mitropoulos

1958–59:

Cavalleria Rusticana (Mascagni): designed by Rolf Gérard, staged by José Quintero, conducted by Dimitri Mitropoulos

Pagliacci (Leoncavallo): designed by Rolf Gérard, staged by José Quintero, conducted by Dimitri Mitropoulos

Macbeth (Verdi): designed by Caspar Neher, staged by Carl Ebert, conducted by Erich Leinsdorf

Wozzeck (Berg): designed by Caspar Neher, staged by Herbert Graf, conducted by Karl Boehm

1959–60:

Il Trovatore (Verdi): designed by Motley, staged by Herbert Graf, conducted by Fausto Cleva

Le Nozze di Figaro (Mozart): designed by Oliver Messel, staged by Cyril Ritchard, conducted by Erich Leinsdorf

The Gypsy Baron (J. Strauss): designed by Rolf Gérard, staged by Cyril Ritchard, conducted by Erich Leinsdorf

Tristan und Isolde (Wagner): designed by Teo Otto, staged by Herbert Graf, conducted by Karl Boehm

Fidelio (Beethoven): designed by Horace Armistead, staged by Herbert Graf, conducted by Karl Boehm

Simon Boccanegra (Verdi): designed by Frederick Fox, staged by Margaret Webster, conducted by Dimitri Mitropoulos

1960–61:

Nabucco (Verdi): designed by Teo Otto and Wolfgang Roth, staged by Günther Rennert, conducted by Thomas Schippers

L'Elisir d'Amore (Donizetti): designed by Robert O'Hearn, staged by Nathaniel Merrill, conducted by Fausto Cleva

Alcestis (Gluck): designed and staged by Michael Manuel, conducted by Erich Leinsdorf

Martha (Flotow): designed by Oliver Smith and Motley, staged by Carl Ebert, conducted by Nino Verchi

Turandot (Puccini): designed by Cecil Beaton, staged by Yoshio Aoyama and Nathaniel Merrill, conducted by Leopold Stokowski

1961–62:

Un Ballo in Maschera (Verdi): designed by Ita Maximowna, staged by Günther Rennert, conducted by Nello Santi

1962–63:

Die Meistersinger von Nürnberg (Wagner): designed by Robert O'Hearn, staged by Nathaniel Merrill, conducted by Joseph Rosenstock

Ariadne auf Naxos (R. Strauss): designed by Oliver Messel, staged by Carl Ebert, conducted by Karl Boehm

Adriana Lecouvreur (Cilèa): designed by Carlo Maria Cristini after Camillo Parravicini, staged by Nathaniel Merrill, conducted by Silvio Varviso

La Sonnambula (Bellini): designed by Rolf Gérard, staged by Henry Butler, conducted by Silvio Varviso

Otello (Verdi): designed by Eugene Berman, staged by Herbert Graf, conducted by George Solti

1963–64:

Aïda (Verdi): designed by Robert O'Hearn, staged by Nathaniel Merrill, conducted by George Solti

Manon (Massenet): designed by Ita Maximowna, staged by Günther Rennert, conducted by Thomas Schippers

The Last Savage (Menotti): designed by Beni Montresor, staged by Gian Carlo Menotti, conducted by Thomas Schippers

Falstaff (Verdi): designed and staged by Franco Zeffirelli, conducted by Leonard Bernstein

1964–65:

Lucia di Lammermoor (Donizetti): designed by Attilio Colonnello, staged by Margherita Wallmann, conducted by Silvio Varviso

Samson et Dalila (Saint-Saëns): designed by Robert O'Hearn, staged by Nathaniel Merrill, conducted by George Prêtre

Les Sylphides (Chopin): designed by Rolf Gérard, chore-

ography by Michel Fokine, conducted by Silvio
Varviso

Salome (R. Strauss): designed by Rudolf Heinrich,
staged by Günther Rennert, conducted by Karl
Boehm

1965–66:

Faust (Gounod): designed by Jacques Dupont, staged by
Jean-Louis Barrault, conducted by Georges Prêtre

The Queen of Spades (Tchaikovsky): designed by Robert
O'Hearn, staged by Henry Butler, conducted by
Thomas Schippers

1966–67:

Antony and Cleopatra (Barber): designed and staged by
Franco Zeffirelli, conducted by Thomas Schippers

La Gioconda (Ponchielli): designed by Beni Montresor,
staged by Margherita Wallmann, conducted by
Fausto Cleva

La Traviata (Verdi): designed by Cecil Beaton, staged by
Alfred Lunt, conducted by Georges Prêtre

Die Frau ohne Schatten (R. Strauss): designed by Robert
O'Hearn, staged by Nathaniel Merrill, conducted
by Karl Boehm

Elektra (R. Strauss): designed by Rudolf Heinrich,
staged by Herbert Graf, conducted by Thomas
Schippers

Lohengrin (Wagner): conceived and designed by Wie-
land Wagner, staged by Peter Lehmann, conducted
by Karl Boehm

Peter Grimes (Britten): designed by Tanya Moiseiwitsch,
staged by Tyrone Guthrie, conducted by Colin
Davis

Die Zauberflöte (Mozart): designed by Marc Chagall, staged by Günther Rennert, conducted by Josef Krips

Mourning Becomes Electra (Levy): designed by Boris Aronson, staged by Michael Cacoyannis, conducted by Zubin Mehta

1967–68:

Roméo et Juliette (Gounod): designed by Rolf Gérard, staged by Paul-Emile Deiber, conducted by Francesco Molinari-Pradelli

Hansel and Gretel (Humperdinck): designed by Robert O'Hearn, staged by Nathaniel Merrill, conducted by Franz Allers

Die Walküre (Wagner): designed by Günther Schneider-Siemssen and George Wakhevitch, staged and conducted by Herbert von Karajan

Carmen (Bizet): designed by Jacques Dupont, staged by Jean-Louis Barrault, conducted by Zubin Mehta

Luisa Miller (Verdi): designed by Attilio Colonnello, staged by Nathaniel Merrill, conducted by Thomas Schippers

1968–69:

Tosca (Puccini): designed by Rudolf Heinrich, staged by Otto Schenk, conducted by Francesco Molinari-Pradelli

Das Rheingold (Wagner): designed by Günther Schneider-Siemssen and George Wakhevitch, staged and conducted by Herbert von Karajan

Der Rosenkavalier (R. Strauss): designed by Robert O'Hearn, staged by Nathaniel Merrill, conducted by Karl Boehm

Il Trovatore (Verdi): designed by Attilio Colonnello, staged by Nathaniel Merrill, conducted by Zubin Mehta

1969–70:

Cavalleria Rusticana (Mascagni): designed and staged by Franco Zeffirelli, conducted by Leonard Bernstein

Pagliacci (Leoncavallo): designed and staged by Franco Zeffirelli, conducted by Fausto Cleva

Norma (Bellini): designed by Desmond Heeley, staged by Paul-Emile Deiber, conducted by Richard Bonynge

1970–71:

Orfeo ed Euridice (Gluck): designed by Rolf Gérard, staged and choreographed by Milko Sparemblek, conducted by Richard Bonynge

Parsifal (Wagner): designed by Robert O'Hearn, staged by Nathaniel Merrill, conducted by Leopold Ludwig

Fidelio (Beethoven): designed by Boris Aronson, staged by Otto Schenk, conducted by Karl Boehm

Werther (Massenet): designed by Rudolf Heinrich, staged by Paul-Emile Deiber, conducted by Alain Lombard

1971–72:

Der Freischütz (Weber): designed and staged by Rudolf Heinrich, conducted by Leopold Ludwig

Tristan und Isolde (Wagner): designed by Günther Schneider-Siemssen, staged by August Everding, conducted by Erich Leinsdorf

Pelléas et Mélisande (Debussy): designed by Desmond Heeley, staged by Paul-Emile Deiber, conducted by Colin Davis

La Fille du Régiment (Donizetti): designed by Anna Anni and Marcel Escoffier, staged by Sandro Sequi, conducted by Richard Bonynge

Otello (Verdi): designed by Franco Zeffirelli and Peter Hall, staged by Franco Zeffirelli, conducted by Karl Boehm

281

Bing, Ernst, 84
Bing, Ilka, 219–21
Bing, Nina, 51–52, 75–82, 88,
177, 202, 217, 219–20,
222, 229, 232, 233, 237
Bing, Robert, 84, 91
Bjoerling, Jussi, 132, 149
Blegen, Judith, 46, 214
Bliss, Anthony, 27–29, 54, 81
Boehm, Dick, 63–64
Boehm, Karl, 33, 46, 51, 213,
228
Bohème, La, 56, 130, 151, 174,
196, 201, 212
Bonynge, Richard, 46, 51, 213
Britten, Benjamin, 152, 176
Brodzky, Vava, 177
Bronson, Faith, 64
Brook, Peter, 237
Brooklyn College, 61–62,
66–67, 75
Bubbles (Sills), 65
Bumbry, Grace, 50, 119, 213

Caballé, Montserrat, 50, 65,
130
Caldwell, Sarah, 70–71
Callas, Maria, 16, 62, 63,
95–118, 204, 214
Carlisle, Kitty, 172
Carmen, 150, 169, 203, 213, 214
Carnegie Hall, 97
Cassidy, Claudia, 16, 222
Cavalleria Rusticana, 170, 213
CBS, 196
Chagall, Marc, 175–79, 237
Chapin, Schuyler, 53, 55
Chaplin, Charlie, 169
Chicago Tribune, 222
Chookasian, Lili, 46

Chotzinoff, Samuel (NBC
executive), 196–97
Churchill, Winston, 204
City Center, 34, 111–12
Cleva, Fausto, 212, 213
Cocteau, Jean, 104
Collier, Marie, 214
Collins, Janet, 120
Columbia Artists Management,
54, 67–70, 78, 81,
185–86
Columbia University, 122
Conner, Nadine, 133
Corelli, Franco, 23, 50, 51, 100,
119, 187, 204, 213, 214
Corena, Fernando, 50, 212
Così Fan Tutte, 135
Cossotto, Fiorenza, 130, 214
Crespin, Régine, 50–51, 130,
214
Cross, Milton, 200

Dalis, Irene, 51, 130, 212
Dallas Opera Company,
109–11, 117
Daughter of the Regiment, The, 46
Davis, Colin, 33, 46
De Los Angeles, Victoria, 169
Deiber, Paul-Emile, 46, 213
Del Monaco, Mario, 132
Della Casa, Lisa, 131, 149
Dexter, John, 54–56
Dickens, Charles, 217
Dido and Aeneas, 63
Di Giuseppe, Enrico, 51
Doherty Foundation, 179
Domingo, Placido, 50, 119, 214
Don Carlo, 49, 120, 131,
143–44, 160, 172, 196,
213, 223